Cambridge Elements

Elements in Politics and Society in Southeast Asia
edited by
Edward Aspinall
Australian National University
Meredith L. Weiss
University at Albany, SUNY

RETHINKING COLONIAL LEGACIES ACROSS SOUTHEAST ASIA

Through the Lens of the Japanese Wartime Empire

Diana S. Kim
Georgetown University

CAMBRIDGE
UNIVERSITY PRESS

Shaftesbury Road, Cambridge CB2 8EA, United Kingdom

One Liberty Plaza, 20th Floor, New York, NY 10006, USA

477 Williamstown Road, Port Melbourne, VIC 3207, Australia

314–321, 3rd Floor, Plot 3, Splendor Forum, Jasola District Centre, New Delhi – 110025, India

103 Penang Road, #05-06/07, Visioncrest Commercial, Singapore 238467

Cambridge University Press is part of Cambridge University Press & Assessment, a department of the University of Cambridge.

We share the University's mission to contribute to society through the pursuit of education, learning and research at the highest international levels of excellence.

www.cambridge.org
Information on this title: www.cambridge.org/9781009671484

DOI: 10.1017/9781009070942

© Diana S. Kim 2025

This publication is in copyright. Subject to statutory exception and to the provisions of relevant collective licensing agreements, no reproduction of any part may take place without the written permission of Cambridge University Press & Assessment.

When citing this work, please include a reference to the DOI 10.1017/9781009070942

First published 2025

A catalogue record for this publication is available from the British Library

ISBN 978-1-009-67148-4 Hardback
ISBN 978-1-009-06846-8 Paperback
ISSN 2515-2998 (online)
ISSN 2515-298X (print)

Cambridge University Press & Assessment has no responsibility for the persistence or accuracy of URLs for external or third-party internet websites referred to in this publication and does not guarantee that any content on such websites is, or will remain, accurate or appropriate.

For EU product safety concerns, contact us at Calle de José Abascal, 56, 1°, 28003 Madrid, Spain, or email eugpsr@cambridge.org

Rethinking Colonial Legacies across Southeast Asia

Through the Lens of the Japanese Wartime Empire

Elements in Politics and Society in Southeast Asia

DOI: 10.1017/9781009070942
First published online: March 2025

Diana S. Kim
Georgetown University
Author for correspondence: Diana S. Kim, dk936@georgetown.edu

Abstract: This Element explores the significance of the Japanese wartime empire's occupation of Southeast Asia during World War Two for understanding the region's colonial legacies. It conceptualizes the occupation as a critical juncture that mediated the survival of American and European colonial institutions, and comparatively describes how, between 1940 and 1945, a wide variety of formal institutions for governing territories and people operated under the Japanese, who selectively kept or changed the existing arrangements of their Western predecessors, while sometimes introducing new ones altogether. The Japanese occupation, as such, generated different processes for transmitting pre-1940 colonial institutions into postwar and independent Southeast Asia. Building on new histories of the occupation, this Element offers an analytical framework that helps social scientists specify the mechanisms through which the long-run consequences of colonial institutions obtain in the context of Southeast Asia, while grappling more generally with what constitutes a meaningful rupture to historical continuity.

Keywords: Japanese occupation, colonial legacies, Southeast Asia, empire, critical juncture

© Diana S. Kim 2025
ISBNs: 9781009671484 (HB), 9781009068468 (PB), 9781009070942 (OC)
ISSNs: 2515-2998 (online), 2515-298X (print)

Contents

1 Introduction   1

2 Two Overviews of the Japanese Wartime Empire across Southeast Asia, 1940–1945   12

3 Varieties of Wartime Institutions   28

4 Conclusion   45

References   48

1 Introduction

For centuries, Southeast Asia was ruled by Western colonial powers. Then, between 1940 and 1945, there was a changing of the colonial guard during World War Two. The Japanese replaced the French in today's Cambodia, Laos, and Vietnam, the Americans in the Philippines, the British in Brunei, Malaysia, Myanmar, Singapore and parts of Papua New Guinea, the Dutch in Indonesia as well as the Portuguese in East Timor. And when the war ended, the old Western colonizers returned.

The in-between period, conventionally known as the Japanese occupation, is important for understanding the legacies of colonialism across Southeast Asia today. The ideological bases and discourses through which a new empire made claims to political legitimacy changed, with a self-avowed Asian imperial power professing to liberate fellow Asians from the yoke of European and American rule. New coercive, extractive, regulatory, and documentary institutions for ordering colonial societies and economies emerged, while in some places, territorial and administrative boundaries changed. The Japanese occupation was also a time of heightened emotions, great material losses and gains, as well as extraordinary physical, sexual, and symbolic violence. In retrospect, it is an era that people living in Southeast Asia remember in different ways, ranging from the acute hardships and deprivations of war and the indignities of a double occupation to a turning point towards independence and the birth of new nations.

While the Japanese occupation has long been a subject of rich inquiry for specialists of Southeast Asia, it has not been well-integrated into social scientific inquiries about colonial legacies. It is often sidestepped when scholars analyze the long-run consequences of American and European colonial institutions upon contemporary outcomes, not least because the years of Japanese rule seem so short compared with how long the Western empires prevailed.

This Element addresses this gap. It focuses squarely on the Japanese occupation, conceptualizing it as a critical juncture that mediated the survival of American and European colonial institutions during World War Two. It shows how, between 1940 and 1945, local agents of wartime empires stationed across the region implemented projects for military colonial governance that selectively kept or changed existing institutions, while sometimes introducing new ones altogether, which generated different processes for transmitting pre-1940 colonial institutions into post-World War Two, independent Southeast Asia. This Element as such, offers an analytical framework that helps scholars specify the mechanisms through which the long-run consequences of colonial institutions obtain, while grappling more generally with what constitutes a meaningful rupture to historical continuity.

1.1 Colonial Legacies across Southeast Asia

Colonial legacies constitute a dynamic field of interdisciplinary inquiry.[1] Social scientists seek to explain the impact of foreign rule upon a colonized people, assessing the weight of history upon the present. How did the imposition of new systems of political governance, economic, and social organization affect a country in the long run? Did colonialism influence the emergence and durability of democracies and authoritarian regimes across the world today? Did extractive institutions built by alien rulers help or hinder economic development? Can past imperial ways of drawing territorial boundaries and categorizing people help explain contemporary patterns of interstate conflict or violence along ethnic, racial, and religious lines? Do memories of past losses of sovereignty and precedents of anti-colonial resistance still matter for people's identities and the meaning of nationhood?

Southeast Asia represents a rich site for addressing such questions from a comparative perspective. Between the nineteenth and mid twentieth centuries, the region was divided among multiple imperial powers that conquered territory, built colonial states, and extractive economies as well as modernizing regimes of knowledge.[2] Cross-empire differences provide opportunity for scholars to explore if and how differences in metropolitan politics and ideologies shaped the design and staying power of colonial institutions. Also, a patchwork quilt-like quality to how colonies were administered generate rich subnational variations that are helpful for mapping how, and explaining why, countries colonized by the same national empire, or different territories within the same country, fared differently over time.

Colonial history has left many imprints upon societies throughout Southeast Asia. Foreign classifications of people by race, ethnicity, and religion linger as official naming practices, invented traditions, and documentation regimes that continue to define and reify group identities, while fiscal and coercive institutions that utilized such colonial categories endure and spur communal tensions, intergroup conflict as well as violence throughout the region (Goscha, 2009; Bertrand and Laliberté, 2010; Saada, 2012; Fanselow, 2014; Manickam, 2014; Menchik, 2014; Tajima, 2014; Ferguson, 2015; Hussin, 2016; Cheesman, 2017; Jaffrey, 2019; Pelletier, 2019; Liu and Selway, 2021; Kuipers, 2022; Masucol, Jap, and Liu, 2022). Colonial laws and policies for policing intimacy, regulating familial and religious life, as well as social control have shaped demographic

---

[1] For lucid reviews of recent scholarship on colonial legacies mostly in political science and economics, but also anthropology, history, and sociology, see Thomas and Thompson, 2014; De Juan and Pierskalla, 2017; Simpser, Slater, and Wittenberg, 2018; Kohli, 2020: 1–19; Reyes, 2021; Cirone and Pepinsky, 2022; Naseemullah, 2022: 235–249; Go, 2024.

[2] For a succinct overview, see Aung-Thwin (2005).

imbalances, gender norms, as well as the nature of, and contestation over, jurisdictional boundaries defining personal, public, and political life, while colonial modalities for organizing and representing space undergird today's nation-state forms and territorial borders (Edwards, 2006; Loos, 2008; Ikeya, 2011; Walker, 2012; Firpo, 2016; Sani, 2019). Modernizing projects seeking to mold the minds and bodies of Southeast Asian people through Westernized education, public health interventions, and moral crusades affect present-day attitudes towards medicine, disease, as well as trust in governments (Aso, 2013; Edington, 2016; Li, 2017; Monnais, 2019; Mendoza, 2021).[3]

Today's Southeast Asian economies and state-business relations also bear the weight of the colonial past in the forms of its roads, railways, and other types of large-scale infrastructure that were aimed at resource extraction as well as patterns of migrant settlement and capitalist class formation (Hutchcroft, 1988; Booth, 2007; Vu, 2010; Pepinsky, 2016; Dell and Olken, 2020; Huff, 2020; Rithmire, 2023). Plantations in former Dutch Sumatra, French Indochina, and the American Philippines for sugar, rubber, teak, and other export-oriented commodities were tied to the postindependence rise of labor unions and squatter movements, trajectories of industrialization, as well as famines, disease ecologies, and environmental destruction (Stoler, 1985; Gunn, 2014; Booth and Deng, 2017; Aso, 2018). Corporate entities ordering rich mines and oil fields in former British Burma and Malaya, Dutch-ruled Borneo and West Papua established legal and informational infrastructures that would sustain vexed enclaves, which would at once help propel postindependence national economies while paving the ways for new imperial forms of racial and economic domination (White, Barwise, and Yacob, 2020; Kusumaryati, 2021; Chao, 2023). The city of Yangon retains vestiges of British urban planning schemes for satellite towns, public housing, and land reclamation (Sugarman, 2018). Dalat, now a major tourist destination, was once a remote highland hill station that the French transformed into a "colonial nursery" and spa town for colonists to escape the taxing lowland climate (Jennings, 2011: 173). The strength of business elites in Vietnam, the weakness of local entrepreneurship and banking sector in Myanmar, and the structure of Cambodia's real estate market have been associated with the nature of colonial state intervention and protectionist policies that embraced ethnic favoritism, especially towards Chinese capitalists (Brown, 2011; Sasges and Cheshire, 2012; Nam, 2020).

---

[3] Discussions of colonial legacies relating to Thailand are complicated by disagreements over how to characterize the experience of the Kingdom, which was not formally colonized by Western empires, ranging from scholars who elucidate "traces of the colonial" throughout its politics, legal structure, and economy to those who center attention on Thailand's own internal colonialisms. See Thongchai (1994), Harrison and Jackson (2009), Bowie (2010), Herzfeld (2017), Chakrabarty, Harrison, and Jackson (2018), and Loos (2018).

Moreover, the legacies of colonial rule weigh upon Southeast Asian politics. This is a region with a combination of democratic and authoritarian regime types of varying degrees of strength and durability that scholars have traced back to different colonial institutions for political representation, ways of assimilating ethnic entrepreneurs, dividing and conquering indigenous elites, policing resistance, distributing resources, as well as the experiences of anti-colonial national movements, armed organizations and their leaders (Hedman and Sidel, 2000; Sidel, 2008; Slater, 2010; Kuhonta and Truong, 2020; Weiss, 2020; Mukoyama, 2020; Fibiger, 2023). Southeast Asian states also have varying levels of coercive, punitive and extractive capacity with origins in colonial security apparatuses and fiscal strategies, while the official languages, religions, and various regimes of symbolic knowledge that states adopt today also bear the imprints of colonial pasts (Liu, 2015; Hussin, 2016; Leow, 2016; Rafael, 2016; Nguyen, 2017; Laitin and Ramachandran, in press). Many of today's legal administrative categories are inheritances of colonial laws and policies for education, language, religion, migration, mapping, and border control (Callahan, 2003; Chua, 2003; Tagliacozzo, 2005; Edwards, 2006; McCoy, 2009; Vu, 2010; Lewis, 2012; Amrith, 2013; Cheesman, 2016; Kim, 2020; Sidel, 2021; Dulay, 2022; Ramnath, 2023).

1.2 Why the Japanese Occupation?

For specialists of Southeast Asia, the Japanese occupation has been long recognized as a watershed moment for the region's end of colonial rule and turn to independence. Joyce Lebra's (1977) pioneering analysis of Japanese-trained armies showed how a new generation of military elites emerged during this period, with lasting repercussions for postcolonial politics and state-society relations, as Mary Callahan's (2003) landmark study of the Burmese military authoritarian regime's stubborn persistence has shown with particular clarity. The birth of modern Malaysia, as Tim Harper (1999) has demonstrated powerfully, can be historically narrated by starting with the aftermath of the occupation and war when "a struggle began for the soul of Malaya" (55). Foundational studies on the origins of Southeast Asia's anti-colonial nationalisms have highlighted how the shock of witnessing an Asian imperial power defeat American and European rulers helped ignite new forms of political consciousnesses, mobilizational energy, as well as forceful commitments to resistance and revolution on a popular level (Kahin, 1952; Elsbree, 1953; Benda, 1958; Guyot, 1966; Nitz, 1984; Gunn, 1988; Rafael, 1991; Marr, 1980; Cheah, 2012). "It was not until the Japanese period that nationalism spread deeply into small-town and rural Java," wrote Benedict Anderson in *Java in a Time of Revolution* (2006: 18–19), which presaged his writings on nationalism as an imagined community.

Against this backdrop, there is something strikingly contradictory about how the Japanese occupation figures in our understandings of the long-run legacies of colonialism across Southeast Asia. On the one hand, it is possible to sidestep the occupation altogether by assuming a stubborn continuity to the institutions introduced Western colonial rule. On the other hand, it is also possible to treat this period as a radical rupture that bequeathed a dramatically different terrain from which postcolonial politics, economies, and societies would begin.[4]

Such opposing approaches are partly due to the mass destruction of archival records relating to the Japanese empire's activities in Southeast Asia. In August 1945, with the impending defeat of the Axis powers in World War Two, "the Japanese burnt archives and silenced witnesses to their atrocities" (Bayly and Harper, 2005: 459). Not only government records and politically sensitive documents but also the papers of individuals who had worked with local Japanese military administrations were destroyed (Anctil, 2018: 298; Kratoska, 2018: 6). The returning Western colonial powers also contributed to losses of archives relating to occupation-era activities. In Malaysia for instance, the British destroyed surviving Japanese administrative records, and "materials pertaining to banks and estates were taken to the municipal dumping grounds in Kuala Lumpur, sprayed with a chemical to hasten decomposition, and buried" (Kratoska, 2018: 6–7).

Over the past decades, many alternative sources have emerged to address the absence of official archives. Historians have recovered Japanese propaganda, wartime newspapers, memoirs as well as the intelligence reports of Allied forces and trial records that give partial insight into the inner workings of the Japanese empire, along with the writings of and interviews with Japanese former officers and colonial administrators.[5] The memoirs of Allied force commanders and soldiers, as

---

[4] This divide echoes a canonical debate in Southeast Asian studies over whether or not the Japanese occupation marked a watershed moment for the emergence of political leaders and national identities that proved consequential for countries to gain independence from Western colonial rule, and thus, whether the occupation and war constituted a transformative rupture or period of surprising continuity. The accompanying political stakes concerned questions of agency and wartime collaboration relating to whether the Japanese occupation had caused Southeast Asia's independence or merely catalyzed an ongoing process; and how much of the actions of Southeast Asian nationalist leaders, elites, and everyday people had been autonomous or steered by the Japanese. For formative interlocutors to this debate, see Benda, 1972; McCoy, 1980a, 1980b.

[5] During the 1960s, a wellspring of first-hand accounts by Japanese military and civilian authorities, as well as settlers recounting their wartime experiences emerged amidst a shift within Japanese academia that began to move away from treating the occupation as a taboo topic toward a field of scholarly inquiry. See Akashi (2008b) and Shiraishi (2015) on the birth and evolution of Japanese occupation studies in Japan. See McCoy (1980a: 9) for a critique of the problems of overreliance on Japanese accounts of their own activities, especially regarding education, youth mobilization, communication, and propaganda that risk obscuring the extent of "physical abuse, food confiscations, forced labor impressment, mass incarcerations, and staged spectacles of mass slaughter" that abound during the occupation. For records from the International Military Tribunal for the Far East in Tokyo (IMTFE, also known as the Tokyo Trial) and the two

well as American, Australian, and European prisoners of war form a genre of experience-based observations regarding how occupation unfolded on the ground, while collaborative projects for identifying archives that escaped wartime and postwar destruction had enabled the selective recovery of documents from Japanese Military Administrations (JMA).[6] The writings of national leaders and sustained efforts to bring alive the voices of people in Southeast Asia during the occupation through oral histories, memoirs, travel diaries, and interviews as well as occupation-era newspapers have generated valuable glimpses into the microlevel inner lives of political and social actors (Ba Maw, 1968; Lim and Wong, 2000; Kintanar et al., 2006; Ooi, 2006; Akashi and Yoshimura, 2008; Dhont, Marles, and Jukim, 2016; Blackburn 2019; Tsuda, 2020). Drawing on these sources, a wealth of political, economic, and social histories illuminate the dynamism of state-society relations, political economy, and ideas during the occupation, addressing topics that include, but are hardly limited to, wartime legislative activities under the Japanese, and both top-down policies and bottom-up responses towards official language, education, religion, ethnic relations, industrialization, banking, food supply, and labor mobilization (Ikehata and Jose, 1999; Gotō, 2003; Leow 2016; Saito, 2017; Kratoska, 2018; Mark, 2018; Yellen, 2019; Anamwathana, 2020; Huff, 2020a; Laffan, 2021; Eaton, 2023; Ramnath, 2023).

Such enriched archives and histories of the Japanese occupation have not yet been well-integrated into the ways that social scientists study the long-run consequences of colonial institutions in Southeast Asia. For one, recovered records remain partial and seldom contain the type of fine-grained data on variations over time or by place that are necessary for strong quantitative causal analyses. For qualitative approaches to process tracing, which requires reconstructing precise sequences of events, decision-making processes, and discerning actors' choices and their counterfactuals, the available evidentiary basis is also relatively thin (Collier, 2011; Ricks and Liu, 2018). In addition, while there are many in-depth studies of a single territory that elucidate the context-specific experiences of Japanese authorities, indigenous elites, and local communities, there are relatively few comparative works that

---

Tamura and Toyoda trials, see Drea et al., 2006; Online War Crimes Documentation Initiative, University of Hawai'i, Manoa, Accessed here on August 1, 2024 https://manoa.hawaii.edu/wcdi/trial-records/#fn-1.

[6] On the U.S. Office of Strategic Services' (OSS) intelligence reports dealing with the Japanese in Southeast Asia, see Bradsher, 2006: 386–553. Compiled lists of copies of records of selected documents from various Japanese military administrations include Benda, Irikura, and Kishi, 1965; Rōyama and Takéuchi, 1967; Ōta, 1967; Trager, 1971; Ooi, 1998; Kawashima, 1996; Akashi, 2008a; Huff and Majima, 2018. For helpful summaries of available sources for Indochina and Thailand, see essays in Shiraishi (2015); for the Philippines, see Zaide and Zaide (1990).

systematically describe, let alone explain, patterns of inter- and intra-territory differences and similarities.[7]

The Japanese occupation further recedes from scholarly view because it is a complicated historical event that is difficult to categorize succinctly. In many parts of Southeast Asia, but not all, two empires supplanted each other in quick succession (i.e., from British to Japanese rule, and then back to British rule), but at different times through different processes of transferring official authority. These political transitions overlap with World War Two, which as a regional event in the Asia Pacific theater began unevenly across the region, depending on the nature and timing of the Japanese imperial military's territorial invasion. World War Two was also a global war among empires and states, which ended raggedly as the Japanese emperor's declaration of surrender in August 1945 blurred into the onset of civil wars and revolutions in some, but not all, eventually independent countries. Wartime Southeast Asia is, in turn, nested within the Japanese empire's trans-regional reach into East Asia and the broader Pacific World, which both predates and outlasts the years from 1940 to 1945. The Japanese wartime empire's time in Southeast Asia thus defies both easy periodization and neat categorization. It has been characterized as at once a war, a military occupation, a colonial moment, a new colonial era, an interregnum, a late chapter of Japanese empire, and an interlude within Western imperialism (Benda, 1958; Peattie, 1996; Ooi, 1999; Huff and Majima, 2011: 873; Sasges and Cheshire, 2012; Satoshi, 2018). The occupation as such, is a tricky time for which there is little consensus on whether and how it matters for studying long-run colonial legacies.

1.3 Argument and Approach

This Element aims to bring the Japanese occupation more squarely into the study of colonial legacies across Southeast Asia. It conceptualizes this period as a critical juncture during which a wide range of formal institutions under Japanese purview emerged.[8] Some institutions preserved what already existed under European and American rule and others less so, generating different degrees of connectivity between pre- and post-occupation colonial institutions.

I follow a historical institutionalist approach to a critical juncture as "a situation in which the structural (that is economic, cultural, ideological, and organizational) influences on political action are significantly relaxed for

---

[7] For notable exceptions, see Friend (1988), Tarling (2001), Gotō (2003), Booth and Deng (2017), Huff (2020), and Rithmire (2023). For edited volumes with region-wide coverage, see Goodman (1991), Kratoska (1998, 2002, 2005), Koh (2007), and Loh, Koh, and Dobbs (2013).

[8] Formal institutions, following Helmke and Levitsky (2004), refer to "rules and procedures that are created, communicated, and enforced through channels widely accepted as official" (727).

a relatively short period" (Capoccia and Keleman, 2007: 352).[9] The Japanese occupation constituted a brief period of structural fluidity in the world of empires – European, American, and Japanese alike – in which core ideational frameworks, norms, and practices of twentieth-century imperialism were unsettled. As it overlapped with World War Two, the occupation also temporarily loosened imperial capitalist structures that densely connected metropolitan and colonial markets, reconfiguring the globe into a wartime political economy. A heightened contingency colored the years between 1940 and 1945, during which Southeast Asia saw a boom in wartime institutions for colonial governance under Japanese military authority.[10] Vast varieties of official projects for organizing political, economic, cultural, and social life were launched.

The workings of such projects during the Japanese occupation can be usefully categorized into three processes: the direct transmission, indirect transmission, and non-transmission of Western colonial institutions in place before 1940. In reality, these processes blurred together, in part because most colonial institutions were multilayered and intersected with other types of institutions. However, by separating them analytically, scholars may gain firmer footing into studying Southeast Asia's colonial legacies, especially when tracing causal mechanisms over time and grappling with the question of whether, and if so how, the Japanese occupation mattered for the continuity of Western colonial institutions.

Specifically, when *direct transmission* occurred, an existing colonial institution retained the same form and practices of operation even when radical disruptions to its embedding environment occurred. That is, the Japanese empire's takeover did not have a transformative impact; and the occupation in this instance constitutes a period of institutional resilience. A weaker counterfactual guides *indirect transmission* through which the Japanese drew upon but significantly reconfigured institutions that already existed under Western colonial rule.

---

[9] A critical juncture, following Capoccia and Keleman (2007: 352), does not equal change per se, but rather a period of contingency, which "implies that wide-ranging change is possible and even likely but also that re-equilibration is not excluded." That is, a critical juncture allows for possibility and plausibility of change, but may end without actual change compared with the status quo ante. My processual understanding of institutional interactions is indebted to Mahoney and Thelen (2010). On ongoing advances in historical institutionalism, see Fioretos, Falleti, and Sheingate (2016).

[10] Depending on the territory, the duration of occupation varies, ranging from approximately sixty-one months (for wartime Indochina, beginning with the Nishihara Mission's initial entry into northern Vietnam in July 1940 and ending in August 1945) to thirty-two months (for the American-ruled Philippines, British Malaya and Burma, and the Dutch East Indies, where major invasions began in December 1941 in the wake of Japan's attacks on Pearl Harbor). I treat the region-wide occupation of Southeast Asia as from 1940 to 1945, and elaborate on this periodization in Section 2. In this Element, the names of countries and locations are usually referred to by those used in the postindependence period that are more familiar today. I generally use, for example, Indonesia (rather than the Dutch East Indies), Myanmar (rather than Burma) or Korea (rather than Joseon) in the interest of providing clarity for non-specialists of Southeast and East Asia. When using colonial and occupation-era names, I endeavor to indicate as such (e.g., by referring to "former British Burma" or "wartime Indochina").

Rethinking Colonial Legacies across Southeast Asia

Without the occupation, it is still likely that the latter would have persisted but in different forms, for instance, as less state-directed or with shallower reach into society. Finally, the *non-transmission* of preoccupation institutions gives reason for scholars to pause and ask whether the legacies of colonialism that manifest in independent Southeast Asia are actually attributable to European rule during the nineteenth and early twentieth centuries. For instance, if new institutions were created by the Japanese, through learning or borrowing from metropolitan Japan, sites of earlier Japanese conquest in East Asia and the Pacific Islands or foreign countries, then it is possible that some colonial legacies in this region are better conceived of as the legacies of Japanese wartime rule or post-1945 return of a Western empire (rather than its preoccupation colonial institutions).[11]

On-site agents of wartime empires – mostly Japanese but also those of the retreating and eventually returning Western powers – helped shape these different processes of institutional transmission (or lack thereof). They exercised what I call "situational autonomy" over the implementation of metropolitan and high-level military orders. While the Japanese wartime empire espoused a sweeping vision of a pan-Asian imperial order in which Southeast Asia's diverse territories were assigned various strategic and economic roles, high-level dictates on how exactly to realize Tokyo's visions were often abstract, vague, and contradictory (Lebra, 1977; Duus, 1996; Yellen, 2019).[12] Locally stationed officers wielded considerable leeway over the management of their respective jurisdictions, running state-like entities and making adaptions according to local conditions and wartime exigencies.[13] To be clear, these were hardly rogue military officers or wayward bureaucrats defying superior orders or procedures for decision-making. They were followers, not pioneers, of imperial doctrine; rule-abiding rather than rule-bending individuals who toed the lines of metropolitan dictates and adhered to clear military organizational and disciplinary hierarchies.[14] However, when the voice of the Empire's center was vague and the imperial military establishment was divided,

---

[11] On counterfactuals in critical junctures, see Capoccia and Keleman (2007: 355–357). On the vexed yet unavoidable place of counterfactuals in historical causal arguments, see Bunzl (2004).

[12] A key vision was that of building a Greater East Asia Co-Prosperity Sphere (GEACPS), which I discuss in detail in Section 2.

[13] Following Kimberly Morgan and Ann Orloff's felicitous approach to the "many hands of the state," I understand the state, not as a single political form or abstract structure, but as an amalgamation of institutions and organizations that act upon the world in ways that actors recognize as authoritative, along "multiple scales of governance, [with] multiple and potentially contradictory logics," with varying degrees of penetration into society (Morgan and Orloff, 2017: 3). For similarly nuanced conceptualizations of the state in historical context, see Maier (2023) and Blaydes and Gryzmala-Busse (2023). On the analytical value to "unbundling" the state, see an exemplary account by Suryanarayan (2024).

[14] In this regard, such actors are unlike "street-level bureaucrats" or local agents of administrative states and empires that enjoyed significant discretionary power over local policy decision-making as studied by Lipsky (1980), Adams (1996), Kim (2020), and Hassan (2021).

room for such actors to make choices on the ground opened. And facing strong pressures from superior echelons to make occupation work locally, they turned selectively to the institutions that their predecessors had left behind.

I comparatively describe the three different processes of institutional transmission during the Japanese occupation using several mini-case studies, each of which highlights the situational autonomy of local military and civilian agents of wartime empires. Specifically, I demonstrate direct transmission through the wartime experiences of the Raffles Museum and Library in Singapore and the Commonwealth government system and 1935 Constitution in the Philippines. Indirect transmission is traced through the experiences of youth corps mainly in Vietnam and the Burma Independence Army in Myanmar. Processes of non-transmission are shown through vignettes of transnational institutions for labor mobilization, propaganda squads, and neighborhood associations with a mini-case study of the Endau agricultural settlement in Malaysia. I selected institutions that have been relatively well-studied by area specialists of Southeast Asia and historians of the Japanese empire during World War Two in ways that offer productive opportunities for social scientists to observe how the Japanese occupation may help elaborate causal mechanisms and narratives about long-run Western colonial legacies for this region, especially for outcomes relating to regime durability, coercive state capacity, identity categories, and knowledge production.

Comparative description is a narrative approach aimed at identifying similarities and differences across multiple contexts, by providing detailed accounts of what happened, when, where and how, focusing on the actions, decisions, and likely motivations of actors or entities that are central to theoretically motivated questions. As a type of analytical story-telling, it is especially useful for taming complicated and shifting cross-national, subnational, and multi-scalar variations into a systematic picture, a necessary empirical first step for subsequently developing causal explanations for why such variations occur.[15] I narrate mainly from the vantage point of formal institutions operating during the Japanese occupation, which limits the scope of my analysis to official projects of the military and civil administration between 1940 and 1945.[16] My evidence

---

[15] See Kuhonta (2014), and Simmons and Smith (2021), and Cyr and Goodman (2024) for innovative approaches to historical comparisons in interpretive and qualitative research in political science.

[16] Thus, many informal institutions and non-state actors – such as religious organizations, communal elites, and revolutionary leaders – that figure centrally in foundational studies of the occupation are either absent from or at the sidelines of my narrative, as are major events – such as the famines in Java and Vietnam or anti-Japanese peasant rebellions in the Philippines – that occurred in response to, or as a result of, the formal institutions of occupation. Still, understanding the official "hand" of the Japanese imperial state, I hope, may serve as an anchor for future scholars seeking to systematically map and explain the causes of a broader range of cross-national and subnational variations across occupied

Rethinking Colonial Legacies across Southeast Asia 11

draws from the aforementioned recovered documents that historians and archivists have compiled and translated, as well as published memoirs, and digitized collections of oral interviews, while relying on in-depth secondary literature for each country, mainly in English.[17] When possible, I incorporate the perspectives of individuals who were proximately involved in designing, redesigning, repurposing, discarding, or replacing what their American and European predecessors had left behind. When such information is not available, I use explicitly speculative language (such as "it is likely that") to make clear where the absences in evidence are.

This Element is organized as follows. Section 2 provides a region-wide overview of the Japanese occupation of Southeast Asia. In doing so, it offers a periodization of the occupation based on the Imperial Japanese Army (IJA) and Navy (IJN)'s territorial entry into and formal exit from the region from 1940 to 1945. That is, it lays out the permissive conditions that define when the critical juncture began and ended.[18] Section 3 takes a territory-specific focus to comparatively describe processes of direct, indirect, and non-transmission of pre-1940 Western colonial institutions. In doing so, it centers attention on the role of locally stationed military and civilian agents of the Japanese empire in variably keeping or altering what existed under Western rule, or newly introducing institutions borrowed from metropolitan Japan or other parts of the Japanese overseas empire. That is, it lays out the productive conditions of the critical juncture that enabled varieties of wartime institutional interactions. Section 4 concludes by laying out future research directions for studies of colonial legacies in Southeast Asia.

Southeast Asia. For a more holistic understanding of the occupation, as well as the causes and consequences of major famines, massacres, and social uprisings, I defer to deeply-researched histories that include, but are certainly not limited to Ooi (1999), Tarling (2001), Kerkvliet (2002), Bayly and Harper (2005), Booth (2007), Lanzona (2009), Gunn (2014), Terami-wada (2014), Kratoska (2018), and Huff (2020a, 2020b). For illuminating histories of the post-1945 return of Western colonial powers and varieties of wars, revolutions, and decolonization processes across Southeast Asia, see Reid, (1981), Cheah (1988), Harper (1999), Bayly and Harper (2007), Marr (2013), and Ooi (2013). I offer a comparative analysis of how different types of occupation institutions affected post-1945 political trajectories in a working paper.

[17] In this regard, this Element is an exercise in synthesis and interpretation, which endeavors to bridge between the depth and breadth of two rich bodies of literature – histories of the Japanese wartime empire and occupation in Southeast Asia in mostly Anglophone traditions and social scientific inquiries into the region's colonial legacies – and bring them into conversation. To understand the much wider and equally dynamic scholarship on the Japanese occupation in non-English languages, see Gotō (2003), Namba (2015), Shiraishi (2015) for Japanese and French-language scholarship; in Dutch, Louis de Jong's twenty-nine volume history of the Second World War in the Dutch East Indies (*Het Koninkrijk der Nederlanden in de Tweede Wereldoorlog*) represents a landmark study, a part of which was translated into English (see de Jong, 2002).

[18] Soifer (2012: 1574–1576).

2 Two Overviews of the Japanese Wartime Empire across Southeast Asia, 1940–1945

Southeast Asia was a late addendum to Japan's overseas empire.[19] By 1940, when the IJA started to invade the region, the Japanese empire's reach had already expanded over large swaths of East Asia and the western edges of the Pacific Ocean. It was a large and variegated entity, which comprised many different arrangements for colonial and quasi-colonial rule, ranging from the fully annexed territories of Taiwan (1895) and Korea (protectorate in 1905 and annexed in 1910), Kwantung Leased Territory and the South Manchurian Railway Zone (1905, 1906) to a League of Nations mandate in Micronesia (1919) and various so-called puppet states such as Manchukuo (1932) and the Wang Jingwei regime (1940) in parts of today's China.[20] With the addition of Southeast Asia, the Japanese empire became "one of the largest imperial structures in the modern history of colonialism," encompassing nearly six million km^2 of land, populated by at least 340 million people.[21]

Section 2 traces the contours of Southeast Asia under Japanese rule from 1940 to 1945. This period is conventionally known as the Japanese occupation, as scholars have tended to distinguish the wartime military-led nature of the Japanese empire's takeover of the region from American and European colonialism proper. During these years, Southeast Asia acquired its imagined coherence as a unit of political geography, a region within Asia in its familiar present-day form (Bayly and Harper, 2005: 463). The Japanese during the wartime 1940s referred to Southeast Asia as part of the "Southern Region" or "South Seas."[22] In

---

[19] For excellent overviews of Japan's colonial expansion from 1895 to 1945 that include summary treatments of seminal and recent scholarship, see Peattie (1984), Sand (2014), and Shirane (2022: 4–11). On how preoccupation Southeast Asia figured within the expanding Japanese empire's ideological, geostrategic, economic considerations, see Peattie (1996), Tarling (2001: 1–38), and Clancey (2002). On the preoccupation Japanese imperial presence across Southeast Asia through Japanese settler populations, longstanding trade and commercial networks, and diplomacy and intelligence, see Yu-Jose (1996), Abinales (1997), Ooi (1999), Kwartanada (2002), Shiraishi and Shiraishi (1993), Harper (2007), Clulow (2013), and Tremml-Werner (2015).

[20] On Japan's pre-1895 history of imperial expansion, see Howell, 2005; Uchida, 2016.

[21] Conrad (2014: 6). See Duus (1996) for estimates of the total population of the Japanese overseas empire during World War Two as ranging between 340 million (p. xii) and 440 million (p. xiii, Table 1.1, "Grand Total"), in part because it is difficult to ascertain the number of people in occupied China. Duus estimates the population of occupied Southeast Asia, including Indochina and Thailand, at approximately 146 million individuals.

[22] As Peattie (1996: 190) notes, Southern Region (nampō) and South Seas (nan'yō) were "nebulous terms" that could include Japan's mandate territories in Micronesia (as the "Inner South Seas," uchi nan'yō) and extend to parts of Australia and New Zealand (included in the "Outer South Seas," soto nan'yō). On the long genealogy of Japan's political, military doctrines and practices of southern expansion into Southeast Asia and the Pacific Islands, see Yano (1975), Peattie (1992), and Iwamoto (1999).

tandem, the English-language term Southeast Asia roughly followed the jurisdictional boundaries of the South East Asia Command (SEAC), which had been established in 1943 to oversee the Allied forces' operations in the Pacific Theatre during World War Two.[23]

The Japanese empire's occupation of Southeast Asia involved a multistage, multilayered process of invading the region and establishing schemes for colonial military governance. In a sweeping sense, the Japanese adopted three different approaches to occupation. The first entailed the Japanese jointly ruling with a foreign leader already in power, which prevailed in today's Vietnam, Cambodia, Laos, Thailand, and East Timor. A second approach placed an indigenous leader at the head of a "puppet state" that the Japanese oversaw, which applied to today's Myanmar and the Philippines after 1943. The third approach was establishing a Japanese military-led administrative body, which applied to today's Brunei, Indonesia, Malaysia, Papua New Guinea, and Singapore, as well as Myanmar and the Philippines before 1943.

At one level, such distinctions over who formally held high seats of power were meaningful. At a time of hard military invasion, softer performances of authority in official political arenas could serve both as instruments of self-legitimation (for the occupiers) and as a resource for retaining dignity, sustaining resistance and political survival (for the occupied). Having a nominally independent government served as "a face saving device" for the Burmese, according to U Hla Pe, who worked as Director of Press and Propaganda in Japanese-occupied Burma.[24] For Claro Recto – the influential statesman and judge who served as Foreign Minister in the Second Philippine Republic's puppet government – even as he recognized that "independence was to be the sugar coating to disguise the bitter pill inside," it was also the only viable way to keep a Filipino voice for the people in politics. For, "[n]ot every man, woman and child could go to the mountains and become a guerrillero. If people were to be spared the rigors of direct military rule, there had to be a government by Filipinos."[25] Moreover, Tokyo's wartime politicians and imperial strategists favored signing diplomatic and defense treaties with the leaders of occupied territories. Even as such bilateral agreements were highly unequal and mere fictions of voluntary partnership, in some instances, the Japanese would abide by their terms.[26]

---

[23] Amrith and Harper (2014: 3) and Mitsuomi and Fernando (2014). On the orthographic morphing of the English language version of Southeast Asia as traceable to the U.S. State Department's 1945 creation of its first "Division of Southeast Asian Affairs," see Emmerson (1984: 3, fn6).
[24] U Hla Pe (1961: 14). [25] Recto (1946: 5 and 18).
[26] For instance, Japan's formal recognition of Indochina and Thailand was meaningful, according to Reynolds (1996: 251) in that "treaty relationships made it difficult for the Japanese to operate in the arbitrary, untrammeled fashion to which they had become accustomed."

At another level, these three general approaches to occupation do not map neatly onto the much wider variety of formal institutions that proliferated across Southeast Asia between 1940 and 1945. The region experienced a boom of official projects for colonial military governance, namely, top-down initiatives to manage each invaded territory, its people and resources in order to sustain Japan's war-making and empire-building endeavors.[27] Such projects differed by place, could shift over time, and were also often interconnected but not necessarily centrally coordinated. To understand such finer-grained differences to Japanese occupation approaches, it is necessary to pay attention to the locally stationed agents of wartime empires and the nature of their situational autonomy. These actors help shed light on how highly context-specific formal institutions could emerge, evolve, and sometimes endure over time.

To convey both levels, Section 2 offers two complementing narratives: first, a sweeping bird's eye view of the Japanese empire's invasion of Southeast Asia and establishment of three types of high-level political governing bodies; and second, a more localized worm's eye view of the region's uneven landscape for colonial military governance. Analytically, this section examines the permissive conditions delineating the occupation as a critical juncture in the region's legacies of Western colonial rule, by situating it in broader contexts of the Second Sino-Japanese War, World War Two, and overlapping ideological, economic, and political crises in the global order of twentieth-century empires.

2.1 A Bird's Eye View

The Japanese entered the 1940s at a furious pace as a "total empire" at war, entangled in armed conflicts on multiple fronts.[28] The IJA had been occupying parts of China since the early 1930s, not only bringing the Japanese into conflict with various Chinese armed forces but also spurring border fights with the Soviet Union and Mongolia.[29] By the summer of 1940, when the Japanese empire's military incursions into Southeast Asia would begin, the IJA had further taken over parts of central and eastern China, while off the southern

---

[27] Mark (2018: 211) refers to "a process of military-colonial normalization."
[28] Total empires, to follow Louise Young (1998: 12), refer to "multidimensional, mass-mobilizing, and all-encompassing" empires at the height of industrial capitalism's global expansion that were especially adept at large-scale mobilizations of people and resources in both metropolitan domestic and colonial societies. On Japan's wartime empire from 1931 to 1945, see Duus, Myers, and Peattie, (1996).
[29] For details on the significance of the IJA's occupation of North and Northeastern China, following the Manchurian Incident (1931), see Young (1998) and Mitter (2000). On tensions over Manchukuo's borders with Mongolia and the Soviet Union, see Coox (1985). For an invaluable study of the broader context of Japanese-Soviet relations, see Linkhoeva (2020).

coast, the Imperial Japanese Navy (IJN) occupied Hainan and the Spratly Islands.[30] But the war had since reached a stalemate, not least due to the tenacity of China's resistance forces, most notably, the Kuomintang (KMT)'s army led by Chiang Kai-shek, in the southwestern provinces of the country.[31] Such parts of China brushed against the northern borders of British-ruled Burma and French-ruled Indochina.

These fault lines of the Japanese empire were embedded within several ongoing seismic shifts in the world's imperial order. Western Europe's empires were confronting challenges from anti-colonial nationalist uprisings throughout their colonies that had gained momentum from the First World War's large-scale mobilization of colonized peoples and fraught processes of demobilization, alongside failed promises of self-determination (Manela, 2007; Pedersen, 2015; Minohara and Dawley, 2020). Strident forms of Pan-Asianism that favored the ejection of Western empires were on the rise, marking a shift away from earlier calls for emulating the West and modernizing Asia in its mold (Akira, 1965; Peattie, 1984; Aydin, 2007).

Global norms and rules for economic engagement among imperial powers were also in flux. Worried that the worldwide economic crisis of 1929 and its aftermath portended the collapse of a liberal international order, Western empires were turning against free trade and embracing narrower forms of protectionism in ways that heightened great power rivalries in Asia (Duus, 1996; Young, 2017). Not only did industrializing Japan hunger for more natural resources and markets for manufactured goods than its home islands could support, but it also faced heightened barriers to accessing American and European colonial markets in Asia as Japan's prolonged conflict in China met with weaponed uses of trade interdependence.[32] The Japanese imperial military's resolve to move into Southeast Asia sharpened as the United States began to embargo oil, steel, iron, and other exports to Japan that were important for the latter's industry and war efforts (Tarling, 2001: 49–50; Kratoska, 2018: 2–3).

The outbreak of World War Two in Europe further destabilized the political holds of metropolitan governments over their colonies. For Southeast Asia, the realignment of once rivaling empires into Allied powers unsettled the ways that the American, British, Dutch, French, and Portuguese had long divided control

---

[30] On the IJN's invasion of Southern China, following the Pakhoi Incident (1936), and the eventual occupation of Hainan and Spratly Islands (1939), see Peattie (1996: 216–217). On the role of the Colonial Government-General of Taiwan alongside the Navy, see Shirane (2022: 103–111).

[31] For details on the Japanese military strategic perspective toward Chiang's forces, see Tarling (2001: 39–45). On the broader context of the Chinese Civil War and the regional, global wars in which it was embedded, see Paine (2012).

[32] On weaponized interdependence, see Farrell and Newman (2019).

over the region. The early defeats of France and the Netherlands to Nazi Germany created political vacuums, weakening their ability to defend colonial rule over Indochina and the East Indies (de Jong, 2002; Brocheux and Hémery, 2009). For Japan – a major Axis power and empire armed with assertive ideological claims as an Asian savior that could liberate Southeast Asia from Western imperial domination, in need of resources to fight its multifront battles in East Asia, while also weary and wary of its prolonged war in China – the summer of 1940 was an opportune time to begin invading Southeast Asia.

One of the earliest territorial imprints of Japan's imperial military fell upon Indochina, in today's northern Vietnam. In July 1940, the Nishihara mission – named after the IJA Major General Nishihara Issaku who led a group of around forty Japanese military officers and diplomatic personnel – arrived in Hanoi to secure a blockade against Chiang's forces (Yoshizawa, 1992: 18–21). It established six surveillance posts near the border with China and an intelligence network that "soon acquired strong new overtones as a means of paving the way for the military occupation of French Indochina" (Yoshizawa, 1992: 27).[33] By 1941, Japanese military presence had reached into the southern half of Indochina, with at least 35,000 men on the ground, commandeering airfields, naval bases, and other strategic infrastructure (Tarling, 2001: 53–54; Raffin, 2012: 395).

Such incursions onto Indochina were possible, in part because the French colonial authorities yielded to Japanese demands in order to prevent the full takeover of Indochina. At the time of the Nishihara mission's entry, Paris had just fallen and Georges Catroux – the French Governor General of Indochina appointed under the Third Republic – was in a position of weakness. Catroux and his successor Jean Decoux – an appointee of the new Vichy-based government that served as French Indochina's wartime metropolitan authority – yielded to what Nitz Kiyoko (1983: 332) calls Japan's "armed diplomacy," which took substantive control over wartime Indochina in exchange for recognizing France's claims to colonial sovereignty. This highly asymmetrical arrangement for joint rule between an existing foreign ruler and the Japanese would persist for most of the war until March 1945.[34] Although the Japanese

---

[33] Smith (1978) describes the significance of this entry as marking northern Vietnam as "the first area in Southeast Asia to admit Japanese troops," followed by the Battle of Long Son (September 1940), the first invasion by the IJA (268–272, quote from 268).

[34] On March 9, 1945, the Japanese launched a coup against the French, establishing direct control over Indochina. The IJA 38th Army's head Tsuchihashi Yuitsu replaced Decoux as Governor General of Indochina, and the Japanese attacked, disarmed, and imprisoned French officers and native colonial soldiers, while detaining French settlers. See Marr (1995: 62–63). For details on this event, also known as Operation Meigō Sakusen (Operation Bright Moon), see Nitz (1983), Smith (1978), and Marr (1995: 13–61).

ruled much of Indochina, the Vichy French colonial government kept its seat of power and exercised relative autonomy over some policy issues.[35]

Similar approaches to joint rule occurred in Thailand and East Timor, where the Japanese also kept existing rulers in their official capacity. In the case of Thailand, which had escaped formal Western colonization, attacks in December 1941 upon its southern coast and the entry of Japanese troops in Bangkok pushed its government – led by Prime Minister Plaek Phibunsongkharam, also known as Phibun, who sympathized with a strand of fascist ideology that favored militant forms of irredentist nationalism – to accede to Japanese demands for stationing soldiers and allowing access to Thailand's railways and roads, airfields, naval bases, warehouses, stocks of fuel and ammunition, and communication infrastructures (Reynolds, 1996: 253).[36] In return, Thailand kept its status as a sovereign nation and Thai wartime leaders gained territorial concessions while retaining official decision-making capacities in domestic and foreign affairs, albeit in a highly limited fashion.[37] In the case of Portuguese-ruled Timor, which was invaded by Japanese troops in February 1942, the colonial governor, Manuel d'Abreu Ferreira de Cavalho, remained in office and the Japanese allowed some areas to formally remain under Portuguese jurisdiction.[38]

A second type of approach to Japanese occupation in Southeast Asia involved ousting the existing ruler and installing a new governing body headed by a leader among the colonized, a nominally independent government that substantively answered to Japanese military authorities stationed in the country. Such approaches prevailed in today's Myanmar and the Philippines for part of their occupation. Both experienced full-fledged military invasions by the Japanese that culminated in the surrenders of British and American colonial authorities. Then British Burma fell under the purview of the IJA's 15th Army; and beginning in August 1943, the Burmese lawyer and politician Ba Maw

---

[35] For instance, see Freud (2014) on Vichy economic policy in Indochina; Namba (2012) on cultural policy; Raffin (2005) on youth movements and education. See Brocheux and Hémery (2009, 338–343) for details on what they aptly refer to as a Franco-Japanese state collaboration.

[36] Thailand been forced to cede enclaves on the left bank of the Mekong River to the French earlier in the twentieth century. Phibun embraced an irredentist agenda to recover the "lost territories," which stoked tensions and eventually a border war in January 1941 between Thailand and French Indochina. By way of stepping into broker a truce to end this conflict, the Japanese established a Thai-Japanese state collaboration. On Phibun and the place of fascism in his wartime political agenda for the recovery of Thailand's "lost territories," see Reynolds (2004) and Strate (2015).

[37] For instance, Thailand received what the Japanese referred to as "gifts" of territory, including the Malay States of Kedah, Perlis, Kelantan, and Trengganu (that had been part of formerly British Malaya); the provinces of Battambang, Siem Reap, Sayaboury, and Bassac (that had been part of French Indochina), as well as areas of the Shan States of Keng Tung and Mong Pan (that had been part of British Burma). See Raffin (2005: 122–123, 133–134), Kratoska (2018: 88–93), and Ferguson (2021: 55–56). On the restricted nature of wartime Thailand's financial policies, see Anamwathana (2020), Charoenvattananukul (2020) on limited foreign policy decision-making capacities.

[38] Kammen (2015: 109).

headed a governing body called the State of Burma, which the Japanese declared as independent, with a Burmese-staffed cabinet and its own armed forces (initially called the Burma National Army or BNA).[39] In the Philippines, where the IJA's 14th Army took over, the Filipino judge Jose Laurel sat at the helm of the Second Philippine Republic, inaugurated in October 1943, which had a national assembly with Filipino legislators and their elected speaker.[40]

In the official parlance of the Japanese empire at the time, occupied Burma under the State of Burma and the Philippines under the Second Philippine Republic both achieved independence. For the Japanese, the term independence relating to Southeast Asia had several meanings, all of which were deemed compatible with military invasion. Independence could refer to a fictitious sovereign status accorded to a ruler, foreign or indigenous, with autonomous sources of political authority. To be independent could also mean being freed from Western rule, with the Japanese imperial military as a self-avowed liberating force that was only occupying, not colonizing a territory. In this sense, nearly all of Southeast Asia, as it had been under American, British, Dutch, French, and Portuguese colonial rule had become independent *through* Japanese occupation. Yet another meaning of independence was a so-called gift of autonomy over domestic affairs that the Japanese could confer or a relatively elevated status within Japan's imperial scheme of political hierarchy.

The hollowness of independence in all three senses was evident to those who gained it. "This independence we have now is only a name," Aung San told Ba Maw, even as the former agreed to serve as War Minister for the State of Burma, what he called "a Japanese version of home rule" (Yoon, 1978: 264). Government policies required the approval of Japanese advisers, with the ultimate assent of Kawabe Masakazu, the head of the Japanese forces stationed in Burma at the time. Labels of puppet state, collaborationist government, pro-Japanese regime, satellite regimes or showcase regime conventionally apply to the State of Burma and the Second Philippine Republic in ways that connote an absence of autonomy on the part of their leaders.[41] Yet, as nuanced readings of

---

[39] On the Japanese invasion and occupation of Burma, see U Hla Pe (1961), Guyot (1966), Yoon (1978), Taylor (1980), Naw (2001), and Callahan (2003).

[40] On the Japanese invasion and occupation of the Philippines, see Agoncillo (1965), Steinberg (1967), Goodman (1988), Ikehata and Jose (1999), and Ileto (2007).

[41] The nature of these new governing bodies, especially the extent to which their leadership was complicit, voluntarily or coerced, with the Japanese is a much-debated subject. See Brook (2012) for a powerful reflection on the intertwined empirical and normative stakes of historical inquiry into wartime collaboration for East Asia. For exemplary executions in the context of occupied Southeast Asia, see Cuunjieng (2017) for the Philippines; Keith (2017) for Vietnam; and Yellen (2019) for Burma and the Philippines.

the writings of such leaders have shown, complicity in power did not directly translate into a cooptation of ideas.[42]

Moreover, the formalities of independence that the Japanese accorded to today's Myanmar and the Philippines are meaningful as they contrast with countries where such official recognition was not given at all. In today's Brunei, Indonesia, Malaysia, Papua New Guinea, and Singapore, the Japanese took a third type of approach of establishing fully Japanese-run governments under Japanese military authority throughout the occupation. In general, commanders of the IJA's 16th and 25th Armies and the IJN divided control over three clusters of territory, which did not necessarily follow boundaries drawn under European rule. The 16th Army's commander headed a JMA for the island of Java, which had been part of the Dutch East Indies.[43] The 25th Army's JMA oversaw both Sumatra, another major island of the Dutch-ruled archipelago world, and the formerly British-ruled Malaya and Singapore.[44] The IJN oversaw yet another portion, including the islands of Sulawesi, the western halves of Guinea and Timor, and the southern part of Borneo.[45]

Co-ruling with an existing foreign ruler. Indirectly ruling through an indigenous leader-led government. Or directly ruling through a Japanese officer. Consider these three approaches to occupation – which depended on the identity of who formally sat in high-level positions of power – as a first cut, a way to begin making sense of the complexity of occupied Southeast Asia's institutional terrain.

To be clear, this bird's eye view has several limitations. For one, the three types do not necessarily depict a territory's continuous experience under Japanese occupation. Myanmar and the Philippines were initially under JMAs but shifted to Burmese and Filipino-led governments midway through the war. Indochina's

---

[42] For instance, see Illeto (2004) and CuUnjieng (2017) on José Laurel, who led the Second Philippine Republic. Regarding Laurel's program for "Assertive Filipinism," CuUnjieng (2017: 9) brilliantly shows how it was a product "not only of circumstantial opportunity and the logic of collaboration," but also entailed a vision of a cohesive nation of the Philippine people, which blended racialized nativist ideas with political narratives anchored in the Philippine Revolution in ways that can be read as an intellectual continuation of his prewar political philosophy.

[43] On the Japanese invasion and occupation of Java, see Benda (1958), Sato (1994), and Mark (2018). On Sumatra, see Reid (1975) and Stoler (1985).

[44] On the Japanese invasion and occupation of Malaya, see Akashi (1970), Cheah (2012), and Kratoska (2018). In April 1943, Sumatra was separated from Malaya administratively. See Reid (1981: 22).

[45] In addition, there were several governing bodies under smaller scales of military authority, such as the Borneo Garrison Army's JMA, which oversaw the northern parts of Borneo. Unlike territories assigned to the IJA, the IJN-occupied territories established naval civil administrative offices with a mandate of establishing permanent retention. See Ooi (2011: 39–40). For details on the Japanese invasion and occupation of Borneo, see Hussainmiya (2003), Ooi (2011).

joint rule arrangement between Vichy France and Japan fell apart in March 1945, giving way to full Japanese military rule until the end of the war. Second, a sweeping perspective also lends to simplistic metropolitan-based explanations of cross-country differences that risk overreading a clarity of goals on the part of Japan's imperial war-makers while positing excess coherence to the military planning of Southeast Asia's post-invasion governance. For instance, it may seem that the Japanese deliberately chose joint rule arrangements for countries with Axis-aligned or neutral governments, which include Vichy France, Thailand, and Portugal. Many countries with direct Japanese-run governments were those that had been invaded in the wake of the bombing of Pearl Harbor in December 1941. It is also possible to view the establishment of "puppet governments" as Tokyo's decisions based on the economic value of different territories; Myanmar and the Philippines as seemingly less costly sites for granting nominal independence compared with oil-rich Borneo and Java.

There is a cleanness to such explanations that does not align well with the historical realities that specialists of the occupation have identified. Tokyo's shaky planning for post-occupation governance has been a longstanding theme in histories of the Japanese wartime empire, perhaps best illustrated by high-level confusion over the Greater East Asia Co-Prosperity Sphere (GEACPS).[46] In a nutshell, the GEACPS was the Japanese empire's vision of a pan-Asian order that wove together Japan, Taiwan, Korea, China, Hong Kong, Micronesia, Australia and New Zealand, parts of Russia, Southeast Asia as well as South Asia into a self-sufficient economic bloc with forms of political organization and legitimation claims in opposition to Western imperialism's white racial domination.[47] As part of official discourse, the GEACPS was first announced in August 1940 by the Foreign Minister Matsuoka Yōsuke and it became professed as the core aim of Japan's national policy and imperial expansion throughout the war (Lebra, 1975: 71–72). Core ideas included building an Asia for Asians, united as "eight corners under a shared roof" (hakkō ichiu), and a transnational, pan-regional economic

---

[46] Duus (1996) and Mimura (2011b).
[47] The GEACPS is notoriously difficult to pin down. It has been variably understood as an ideology, a slogan, a legitimation strategy, policy, and program that invoked Japan's manifest destiny for leadership on the basis of racial superiority, a resolve to liberate Asia from the yoke of European colonial rule; a discourse for mobilizing religious sentiments; a counterhegemony to the liberal internationalism of Anglo-American powers; a coordinating network for mobilizing and transferring labor and resources across far flung territories to sustain the Japanese overseas empire; a constellation of ideas and expertise combining "various strands of Japanese technocratic and right-wing thinking" (Mimura, 2011b: 7); a conjunctural critique of Western domination over Asian races, an appeal to pan-Asian solidarity, an alibi for new imperial forms based on racialized hierarchies; a strategic attempt to mirror the United States' Monroe doctrine-style of "sphere of influence" diplomacy. See Yellen (2019: 8–12) for an excellent overview of a voluminous literature on the GEACPS and its contested significance; 50–102, 141–168 on the GEACPS' evolving definition, scope, and role.

order.⁴⁸ Yet it was only *after* the attacks on Pearl Harbor that politicians and policy-makers began to seriously grapple with questions of how Japan's empire would actually operate differently from the white colonizers it had displaced; how to make coexistence and coprosperity work, as well as whither the boundaries of Greater East Asia. As Jeremy Yellen (2019: 77) underscores, "[v]isions for the future and attempts to institutionalize order in Greater East Asia followed the Rising Sun flag, not vice versa." Indeed, as late as February 1942, such confusion over the GEACPS prevailed in discussions at the highest level of decision-making that Prime Minister Tōjō would have to ask his equally nonplussed advisors what exactly was the Coprosperity Sphere (Yellen, 2019: 4 and 78–79).⁴⁹

Clear lines are also difficult to draw between grand strategy or the wartime value of a given territory and its political organization. The Japanese eventually did invade and occupy Portuguese Timor, a decision that was hotly debated among officers of the army and navy, cabinet ministers, international legal advisors, as well as the prime minister and emperor.⁵⁰ The Malay peninsula's natural resources were not necessarily a key factor in the Japanese decision for invasion and indeed, its "tin and rubber industries were a positive liability because these commodities no longer had a market and the large sector of their economy dependent on their production and export could not be sustained" (Kratoska, 2018: 1). Japan's granting of independence to Ba Maw's Burma went alongside recognition of its valuable oil

---

⁴⁸ Economically, one vision of the GEACPS, as Mimura (2011a: 189) shows, was not on the basis of free trade and comparative advantage, "but rather the organic, hierarchical, functionalist principles of totalism and the multilateral business organization in which each member country, according to its ability (kaku minzoku no bun ni ōjite), contributes its raw materials, labor, capital or technological expertise for the benefit of the bloc as a whole." Illuminating studies of categorizations of people and territories within the GEACPS and their political and ideational underpinnings include Morris-Suzuki (1998) and Shirane (2022).

⁴⁹ Regarding Southeast Asia specifically, snapshots of the GEACPS's formal design convey conflicting goals and inconsistent assessments of the value of occupied territories, especially regarding Myanmar. Lebra (1977, 44) demonstrates Tokyo's confusion regarding occupied Burma and its independence in "two nearly simultaneous pronouncements by the same policy-making body: the Imperial General Headquarters-Government Liaison Conference." While on November 15, 1941 the Liaison Conference issued a decision that "the independence of Burma will be promoted and this will be used to stimulate the independence of India," five days later, it was also decided "to avoid any action that may stimulate unduly or induce an early independence movement" in Burma. Immediately after the attacks on Pearl Harbor, a new document submitted to the Liaison Conference of December 12, 1941 laid out a "General Plan of Economic Policies for the Southern Areas," which divided Southeast Asia into two areas: Area A encompassed "Dutch East Indies, British Malaya and Borneo, and the Philippines" while Area B territories were "French Indo-china, Burma, and Thailand," initially placing today's Myanmar among the joint rule territories. See Trager (1971: 38). On the continued ambivalence of Tokyo towards occupied Burma and inner disagreements within the imperial military that delayed the granting of independence until August 1943, see Lebra (1977) and Yoon (1978).

⁵⁰ For details, see Frei (1996). See works by Tsuchiya (2019a, 2019b) that shed welcome light on the significance of the occupation in studies of East Timor and its national histories.

producing capacities.[51] Moreover, the Japanese were promiscuous in establishing mimetic forms of quasi-sovereign status or holding out promises of independence. For instance, in Singapore, the Japanese recognized the Provisional Government of Free India led by Subhas Chandra Bose (Sareen, 2004: 83–84). A spate of formal declarations of independence followed before war's end in 1945, with the Japanese declaring the independence of Laos under King Sisavang Vong (April 8); Cambodia under King Norodom Sihanouk (March 12); and establishing the Empire of Vietnam under Bao Dai and Tran Trong Kim (Raffin, 2005: 194). In Indonesia on August 8, 1945, the Commander in Chief for the Southern Area Army, Terauchi Hisaichi informed the Indonesian nationalist leaders Sukarno and Hatta that the emperor would grant independence before the end of the month, a promise that was never delivered upon (Sluimers, 1996: 34–35).

Moreover, transnational histories of the Japanese empire elucidate the multiple loci for occupation-related policy-making across its overseas territories in ways that complicate any notion of a single metropolitan authority. Highlighting the influence of the Taiwan Colonial Governor-General's office in Japanese imperial expansion into China and Southeast Asia, Seiji Shirane (2022) writes: "Japan's military services did not have a master plan to oversee a multi-front war. Instead, the planning was often piecemeal, messy, and advanced by different Japanese institutional actors who were sometimes at cross-purposes" (104). In Kwantung Leased Territory, as Miriam Kingsberg's (2013) deeply-researched study of the Japanese empire's opium administration shows, formal authority was split among no fewer than four different "'heads,' or branches of government: the Foreign Ministry ... the SMR [South Manchurian Railway Company]; the Kwantung Army; and the Kwantung Bureau," with the latter as operating as a civilian front for the former's military control" (98). Moreover, the Japanese as subaltern imperialists, to borrow Jordan Sand's (2014) apt characterization (as latecomers to the great games of empire and challengers to prevalent understandings of whiteness as hegemony), were "unusually preoccupied with the examples of other empires, which provided models, object lessons and justifications for their own policies," hinting at an inner game of colonial comparisons that complicated the calculations of the imperial war planners (275). Understanding such complexities, and the highly context-specific arrangements for occupying different territories across Southeast Asia, requires a different perspective. Let us now revisit the region from the opposite vantage point, from that of a worm on institutional ground.

---

[51] Trager (1971: 67). On the economic value and preoccupation significance of the Yenangyaung oil fields in global imperial context, see Ren (2023).

2.2 A Worm's Eye View

The landscape of Southeast Asia from 1940 to 1945 was riddled with projects for colonial military governance. Varieties of formal institutions operated under the purview of locally stationed agents of the Japanese imperial military in charge of performing authority, extracting resources, mobilizing supporters, and repressing dissenters. Commanders of the various IJA field armies, their chiefs of staff and ranking officers of JMA headquarters as well as the leadership of administrative bodies under the IJN oversaw sprawling state-like entities over their jurisdictions. They were tasked with executing occupation policies for education, language, religion, information and propaganda, public works, taxation, transportation, food distribution, labor, agriculture, and industrialization, as well as trade and finance (Huff, 2020a). Such work, in turn, relied upon a plethora of lower-ranked officers, soldiers as well as civilian bureaucrats and diplomats – some directly commissioned by the army or navy, others seconded from metropolitan ministries – as well as agents of Japanese corporations, private contractors, and the media. In the employ of a wartime empire, the many individuals that comprised official Japanese presence, as such, blurred boundaries between formal and informal authority, public and private interest drawn during times of peace.

Such actors wielded situational autonomy over the management of an occupied territory. Theirs was a narrowly circumscribed ability that toed the line of metropolitan dictates and followed orders set by superior echelons of the Japanese imperial military. Yet, situations defined as matters of wartime exigency abounded, ranging from worrisome episodes of social unrest – real and suspected – shortages of food and labor, a guerilla attack, or the death of a commander to what the Japanese saw as salutary opportunities for courting elite supporters, mobilizing fighters, raising money, or winning popular hearts and minds. Keeping within the bounds of their formally delegated authority, on-site agents had considerable leeway over the direction and tenor of colonial military governance in their jurisdictions.[52] There are several reasons why.

---

[52] At its apex was the Imperial General Headquarters (IGH), the centralized command that combined high officers of the army and navy. Much of the Japanese empire's wartime formal decision-making took place at the IGH Liaison Conferences (among chiefs of the IJA and IJN general staff, major cabinet ministers, and the Prime Minister), and decisions were approved at the Imperial Conferences (which brought in a broader range of cabinet ministers) over which the emperor presided. Relating to matters for Southeast Asia and the South West Pacific, the IJA's Southern Area Army, initially headquartered in Saigon, had a strong voice, and commanded the five major armies that in turn each had a military headquarters (gunshireibu) each with administrative hierarchies for decision-making. For the IJN occupied territories, initially the Commander-in-chief for the Southwest District Fleet (for Southern Borneo) and later the Second Southern Expeditionary Fleet headed a Naval civil administrative office (minseibu) with a hierarchical structure for local administration. For details on the structure of military administrative hierarchies in IJA and IJN occupied territories, see Benda,

First, metropolitan dictates on how to govern Southeast Asia were often vague enough to encompass multiple possible approaches to local administration. Not only was the amorphous GEACPS slow to be articulated concretely but also, even when the Imperial General Headquarters (IGH) issued practical guidelines to occupying forces, such orders were not necessarily straightforward to execute. For instance, in March 1941, a working group in the IJA's General Staff Office sketched out an anticipatory plan for how to manage Southeast Asia's diverse territories, the basic ideas of which later informed the IGH's general approach upon the region's actual takeover.[53] As much as possible, stressed the army experts, existing administrative structures and government organs should be kept in place. But also, the officers running the JMAs and other Japanese administrative bodies should demonstrate substantive differences from the preoccupation Western colonial rulers. Officers on-site should respect indigenous, folk customs and win popular support but should also reduce contact with the local population and use violence to subdue them. They should appeal to racial, ethnic, cultural, and historical affinities shared between the peoples of Southeast Asia and Japan but also instill respect for status orders and hierarchies that placed the Japanese at the top. Resources should be extracted and markets should be stabilized with minimal effort but also, Japanese control over major industries should be centralized, new currencies should be issued, and financial arrangements restructured. Chinese capital and their socioeconomic networks should be seen warily and coopted but also recognized as essential for the maximization of output for the war effort and thus left alone.[54] Each territory's economy should strive for self-sufficiency but also contribute to a transnational economic order; Southeast Asia should strive both to be a self-sustaining regional autarky and a proper contributing member

---

Irikura, and Kishi (1965: 53–56), Trager (1971: 52–58, 73–82), Ooi (2011: 38–52), Mark (2018: 224–229), and Kratoska (2018: 55–93). The Southern Area Army's headquarters was moved from Saigon to Singapore in April 1943, to the Philippines in May 1944, and in November of the same year, back to Saigon. See Kratoska (2018: 57–58).

[53] Led by Obata Nobuyoshi, this working group's secret study is often referred to as one of the first practical formulations of Southeast Asia's post-occupation governance, and its recommendation to "make use of existing organs of government" informed core IGH guidelines that were adopted at Liaison Conferences, including the "Summary of Enforcement of the Administration in the Southern Occupied Areas" (November 20, 1941) and "General Plan of the Economic Policies for the Southern Areas" (December 12, 1941). See Charney and Naoko (2015: 219–219) and Yellen (2019: 79–80). While an earlier plan put forth in April 1936 from the IJN research committee (the Tainanken, Research Committee on Plans Concerning the South Seas) also articulated plans for invading Southeast Asia, according to Peattie (1996: 215), even as this document "mark[ed] the beginning of a more insistent, if still peaceful, assertion of the 'southward advance' as a national priority," it was less a concrete plan to territorially invade Southeast Asia but more an assertion of the navy's desire to counterbalance the army's dominance in China and Manchuria.

[54] On the contradictions of Japanese occupation policies towards Chinese populations in Southeast Asia, see Akashi (1970), Maekawa (2002), and Mark (2018, 110–113).

to a pan-Asian, trans-regional interconnected sphere for coprosperity. Given such countervailing imperatives, being consistent with Tokyo's general guidelines allowed for many different specific approaches.

Second and relatedly, the occupation of Southeast Asia was an evolving process nested within the Japanese empire's military wins and losses in the broader Pacific theater of World War Two. A key turning point occurred in 1943, with shifts in metropolitan strategic and ideological orientations towards the region, following the IJN's major defeats in the Battle of Midway and Guadalcanal Campaign.[55] Disruptions to shipping and trade that increasingly cut off Southeast Asia from both Japan and the rest of the world intensified tension between pursuits of regional autarky and transnational connectivity (Huff, 2020a: 42–47). The official goals of the GEACPS were also adjusted in 1943, shifting away from claims to build a Japan-dominant imperium comprised of varieties of subordinate polities towards professing to foster a new order among politically equal, cooperative Asian nations, while advancing a counter-discourse to the American and British-led Atlantic Charter in the form of a Japanese-scripted Pacific Charter (Yellen, 2019: 142–164). Such ideational and discursive shifts further complicated top-down guidelines regarding the management of occupied territories, which were already struggling with the accumulated stresses of wartime life. For instance, most of Southeast Asia's preoccupation colonial economies had faced problems of unemployment that continued into the war. This trend was reversed in 1943, from labor surplus to labor shortage, in part because the Japanese needed larger numbers of workers to build large-scale infrastructures for wartime transportation and communication, and also conscripted many Southeast Asians to serve as military auxiliaries (Huff, 2020a: 46). Hunger and inconvenience gave way to starvation and destitution as stocks of consumer goods became exhausted, and manufactured Japanese goods were no longer readily available. Black markets for food and prewar industrial machinery grew. "By 1943, things had changed," remembers the Indonesian novelist Pramoedya Ananta Toer (Vltcheck and Idira, 2006: 56).

Third, the imperial military establishment was mired in fissures, most famously between the IJN and IJA but also due to tensions vis-à-vis various ministries and other colonial government authorities throughout the Japanese empire. In occupied East Asia, an "interservice tug of war for public esteem and fiscal appropriations" divided the military between army and navy lines while the multiplication of garrisons and institutional complexity of the armed forces created sub-imperial forces within (Peattie, 1996: 213; Young, 1998: 47). Such jurisdictional rivalries sometimes extended to Southeast Asia, complicating the

---

[55] On these battles as significant defeats in the global context of the war and turning point for the Allied forces' victory, Iriye (1993, 193–194), Tarling (2001: 100–116), and Bayly and Harper (2005: 219).

work of the local JMAs, which in turn divided over wartime priorities and time horizons for achieving them as well as different interpretations of military doctrine or metropolitan guidelines. Scholars have shown how widely JMA occupation policies could differ based on the personalities of individual commanders, the opinions and networks of their chiefs of staff and other ranking officers, degrees of fidelity to conservative values, factional divides among military personnel, as well as their relationships with the military police (kempeitai), civilian advisors, corporate actors, and local Japanese settler communities (Akashi, 1970; Nakamura, 1970; Yoon, 1978; Kratoska, 1998; Tarling, 2001; Melber, 2016; Mark, 2018; Booth and Deng, 2017; Huff, 2020a). Within a single jurisdiction, multiple chains of command could also coexist, each with microlevel mandates and priorities that were held accountable to different principals.[56]

A glimpse into situational autonomy at work can be seen in the task of formulating Japan's approach to indigenous rulers in Central Java in early 1942, as it fell upon a civilian official named Miyoshi Shunkichirō, who had been seconded to the Java JMA from the Ministry of Foreign Affairs.[57] Miyoshi had a keen sense of the high stakes of the project at hand, which concerned figuring out how to manage populations in ways that minimized social unrest by working through the Javanese princely rulers in four regions that the Dutch had previously recognized as autonomous. "Not only the rulers but the Javanese people as a whole were watching," Miyoshi recalled (Reid and Akira, 1986: 116).

The Japanese officer traveled to Central Java, collected information on local customs, religion, and precedents of Dutch agreements with the Sultanates of Yogyakarta, Surakarta, Mangkunegaran, and Pakualaman, and brought their ministers to the Java JMA headquarters' Bureau for Princely Territories. And he drafted two reports: one recommended keeping the self-governing regions, and the other suggested their immediate abolition. Miyoshi's rationale for doing so offers a helpful illustration of the making of local occupation policy, of how formal decisions relating to projects for colonial military governance could materialize:

---

[56] For instance, Rangoon in early 1942 had "eight functionally autonomous army, navy, and intelligence operations ... vying with each other to establish control," according to Huff and Majima (2011: 871) who note how this fragmented organization of armed authority helped generate latitude for the IJA's Suzuki Keiji to help train the BNA in Myanmar (discussed in detail in Section 3).

[57] Before the occupation, Miyoshi had served in Japanese consulates in the Hague, Surabaya as well as Vice-Consul in Batavia. See Reid and Akira (1986: 113). This account draws from Miyoshi's personal recollections, reprinted in Reid and Akira (1986: 116–120). On Miyoshi's role as as an interpreter and involvement in the PPKI at the end of the occupation, see Anderson (2006: 62–84).

My reports were to be sent to the Japanese government in Tokyo via the Headquarters of the General Southern Army, and the final decision on this matter was to be made by the government in Tokyo. However, many complicated problems were involved in the process of decision-making and implementation. The General Southern Army was divided between the Army and the Navy, and Indonesia was divided into Army-controlled and Navy-controlled areas. Under these circumstances, the implementation of policy differed according to the characteristics of each area, even though the basic policy was shared. To make matters worse, there was much factionalism arising from the struggle for pre-eminence not only between the Army and the Navy but also between all kinds of groups (Reid and Akira, 1986: 117).

Some favored preserving or even elevating the special status of the Javanese rulers, as "similar to that of the pope in the religious arena" (Reid and Akira, 1986: 118). Others argued for change, to end the exceptional treatment that the Dutch had long accorded the Sultanates. For some, the key issue at stake concerned the Japanese empire's treatment of indigenous history and politics. For others, it was about distinguishing Japan's imperial approach from that of its Western predecessor. Opinions further divided over the necessity of consistency with other occupied territories. The IJA's 25th Army in Malaya had opted not to allow special privileges to the Sultan of Johor; and there were over two hundred additional self-governing regions in other parts of the formerly Dutch-ruled East Indies including Sumatra (also under the 25th Army's jurisdiction at the time) and the Outer Islands (under IJN jurisdiction). Some sought to bring Java in line with Malaya; others did not.

If Miyoshi, by way of treading cautiously among divides within the military establishment, recognized multiple ways to achieve an end, his immediate superior Colonel Nakayama Yasuto, the head of the Java JMA's General Affairs Department, helped narrow down these possibilities. Nakayama was a forceful advocate of maintaining the status quo, who responded to Miyoshi's reports "angrily [saying] that abolition [of the indigenous rulers] would be stupid" (Reid and Akira, 1986: 118). Higher authorities in Tokyo and Singapore deliberated. In the end, Japanese occupation policy for Java sided with keeping the four self-governing territories and their rulers, under new formal titles as "Ko" (a term for Prince in Japanese) who ruled over their Kochi (a Princely territory). A set of documents were issued – a general Army order, instructions from the Gunseikan, and an appointment certificate – under the authority of the Commander-in-Chief of the 16th Army, which its then incumbent, Imamura Hitoshi, handed to each ruler during ceremonies of appointment held on different dates in Jakarta, as the Japanese now called the former Dutch-named city of Batavia: "30 July 1942 for the Surakarta ruler, on

1 August for Yokyakarta, and on 14 August for the Mangku Negara and Paku Alam" (Reid and Akira, 1986: 118).

The four rulers seemed relieved but also sometimes disgruntled and confused about their titles, as was Miyoshi who found himself "several times at a loss for an answer when asked by the rulers of Surakarta and Yogyakarta: but, '[w]hat does Ko mean?'" (Reid and Akira, 1986: 120). For this agent of the JMA – who in addition to his research and policy drafting capacity, played a crucial role as an interpreter and communication bridge between Japanese army officers and Indonesian elites – there was also an ambiguity about the status of Java's indigenous rulers vis-à-vis nationalist leaders such as Sukarno and Hatta, which would become a practical problem when gathering all together. Coopting the Indonesian elites was yet another project of colonial military governance, which was not the same as, but linked to, that of placating the indigenous rulers. According to Miyoshi, "we were unable to find a reasonable answer to the question, which of the two parties should stand higher? Thus we had always to arrange ceremonies so that the Princes and the leaders did not side by side" (Reid and Akira, 1986: 120).

Java in 1942 as such, was one moment in a vast constellation of events and decisions that shaped the institutional landscape of occupied Southeast Asia. Situational autonomy captures the ways that figures such as Miyoshi, Nakayama, and Imamura served as local agents that toed the line of metropolitan dictates and followed orders set by higher-ups in the Japanese imperial military, while still wielding much leeway over military colonial governance. When Tokyo's directives were vague and military superiors were divided, room for their agents to make choices at the margins opened. And to make occupation work, they turned selectively to what infrastructures, organizations, rules and procedures the Western rulers had left behind.

3 Varieties of Wartime Institutions

Section 3 comparatively describes a variety of formal institutions that operated during the Japanese occupation of Southeast Asia from 1940 to 1945. Through a series of mini-case studies, it explores official projects for colonial military governance and places them on a spectrum that ranges from those most reliant upon institutions that already existed under Western colonial rule to those least so. During this critical juncture for Southeast Asia's colonial legacies, locally stationed agents of imperial military and civilian bodies exercised situational autonomy over decisions concerning whether to keep or change extant arrangements or create new ones, playing a pivotal role in shaping different processes of institutional transmission.

3.1 What They Kept: Direct Transmission

Some Western colonial institutions weathered the Japanese occupation with remarkable resilience. The experience of Singapore's Raffles Library and Museum illustrates how local agents of the Japanese wartime empire preserved the infrastructures that their predecessors had established. It was first established in 1874, when the British colonial state took over the privately-run Singapore Library and reopened it as a public institution.[58] Into the first half of the twentieth century, the Raffles Library and Museum served as a repository for government archives and copies of major newspapers, while housing rich collections in natural history and archaeology, which George Murray Reith, the author of one of Singapore's earliest tourist guidebooks, *Handbook to Singapore* (1892) lauded as "one of the largest and most comprehensive in the East" (Lee, 2016: 39). Named after Stamford Raffles – the British official known as the founder of modern Singapore – the Library and Museum became prominently located on Stamford Road and boasted a 90-foot-high dome and striking neoclassical architecture (Lee, 2016: 42). For decades, it played important roles in enacting the grandeur of the British empire's civilizing mission, constructing narratives of the origins and legitimacy of colonial rule, as well as internally socializing European populations residing in or sojourning through the city (Han, 2009; Luyt, 2009).

This British cultural institution escaped the destruction that the Japanese imperial military wrought upon many other sites of knowledge conservation throughout the wartime empire.[59] While Tokyo's general orders had been to leave alone the museums, libraries, and scientific collections in occupied territories, metropolitan dictates on how to manage such institutions were vague and looting by Japanese soldiers in the process of invasion was commonplace (Seet, 1983: 78). In occupied Singapore however, such damages were forestalled through a project for "conserv-[ing] local cultural heritage," in the words of a Japanese civilian researcher tasked with its oversight, named Tanakadate Hidezo.[60] A geologist at Tohoku Imperial University in Sendai, Tanakadate had arrived in Singapore on February 17, 1942 two days after the British surrender to the Japanese.[61] The early days of establishing

---

[58] Its precursor was the school library of the Singapore Free School, first established in 1837. See Han (2009) and Lee (2016: 39–41) on the origins and early development of the Raffles Library and Museum.

[59] For instance, Penang Library lost half its collections; libraries in Australia and Polynesia also suffered the removal of books by invading Japanese officers. See Seet (1983: 75 and 78). Perak's Museum Building in Taiping was looted, and its geology collection was decimated. See *Malaya Tribune*, October 23, 1945. For other examples of libracide in territories under the Japanese empire, see Zhao (2003) on Nanjing. But see Shoji (2015: 113–117) for a similar experience of Japanese preservation of the Federated Malay States Museum.

[60] Mabberley (2000: 3) citing Tanakadate's article in *Asahi Shinbun,* April 4, 1942.

[61] Mabberley (2000: 3).

colonial military governance over Syonan-to, as the Japanese renamed Singapore, brought in agents of multiple loci of metropolitan authority, with blurry jurisdictional divisions over administering the new municipality of Syonan-to among the military officers of the 25th Army-led JMA, civilian officials in the offices of the Mayor and Consul-General, as well as administrators within the JMA's various departments. Tanakadate was among a cluster of Japanese scientists that enjoyed the support of Tokugawa Yoshichika – also known as the Marquis Tokugawa, who was a relative of the Japanese Emperor and would serve as a military adviser for occupied Malaya – and he also had old friendship ties with the 25th Army's Commander (Corner, 1981). Perhaps it was a form of patronage stemming from the personal interests of the royal family in biology; perhaps it was a reflection of an inner power struggle. In September 1942, the Raffles Library and Museum, combined with the Singapore Botanic Gardens, was moved out of the JMA's Food Control Office and became a sub-section of the Syonan-to Muncipality's Department of Education, which according to Seet (1983), gave the "Marquis [Tokugawa] absolute autonomy in policy-making, and he was assisted in the area by Tanakadate until the end of 1942" (84).[62] Tanakadate became the first wartime Director of the Raffles Library and Museum.

Continuities between the British colonial institution and its Japanese wartime counterpart were enabled by collaborative ties forged between Japanese scientists affiliated with the military administration and British administrators who remained in occupied Singapore.[63] Tanakadate worked closely with E. J. H. Corner, a biologist and botanist who had been an Assistant Director for the Botanic Gardens before the war. Together, recalled Corner, he and Tanakadate had hurriedly posted "Do not enter" signs at the entrance of the Library and Museum, which prevented looters and Japanese military officers from destroying its collections. Corner hid copies of newspapers in the Botanic Garden's specimen cabinets, thinking "the only written record, however propagandist and fallacious it might of the Occupation, would be the newspapers" (Corner, 1981: 151). Neither Tanakadate nor Corner were alone in their decisions and ability to sustain the institution. The former, for instance, relied upon the Custodian of Enemy Property, a former employee of the Japanese Embassy

---

[62] On the linked fate of the Singapore Botanic Gardens to the Library and Museum, see "The Singapore Botanic Garden During 1941–1946" in the Garden's Bulletin of Singapore (1947).

[63] The motivations and locus of initiative for this partnership has been a subject of controversy, not least because of accusations of Corner's collaboration as immoral and the whitewashing of imperial Japan's role in wartime Singapore. There is disagreement over whether the initiating authority was the British ex-Governor Shenton Thomas or the Emperor of Japan; the significance of Tanakadate's ties with Yamashita; as well as Corner's status (as attached to the Fruits and Vegetables Section, with the Raffles Library and Museum formerly under the Food Control Office, and as escaping internment in Changi Prison due to an incapacitating monkey bite) and the nature of his relationship with Tanakadate (as a subordinate or friend; the voluntary versus coerced nature of his cooperation). See Seet (1983) Mabberley (2000), and Lee (2016).

in London, for authorization to repair damage to the building's roof and to collect books from the libraries of evacuated British government offices and private collections, which in turn were transported by military lorry-drivers who "would call sporadically at the Raffless [sic] Library ... gesticulating wildly that there were books to be unloaded" (Seet, 1983: 82). Other Japanese scientists visiting Singapore also took interest in the Library, Museum, and Gardens, which continued to operate even after Tanakadate left Singapore in mid-1943 under his successor Koriba Kwan, a professor of Botany at Kyoto Imperial University.[64]

Microlevel ties between local agents of the Japanese empire and British colonial administrators, as such, helped the Raffles Library and Museum survive the war. To be sure, the institution suffered many losses to its collections.[65] However, the day-to-day operations of this institution continued. In terms of the tasks that the library's clerks performed, it felt "more or less the same," according to one man who had worked under both the British and Japanese head librarians.[66] Staff members from the Syonan-to Municipality's Department of Information (which developed propaganda for the Japanese invasion of India and Australia) utilized the library's collections. Books were also circulated to civil internees kept at the Customs House and prisoners-of-war in Singapore's Changi Prison (Seet, 1983: 83). The Museum's central hall became a temporary resting place for the commemorative statue of Stamford Raffles, which was moved off the streets, away from the eyes of Japanese military officers who contemplated its destruction (Corner, 1981: 586).

When the occupation ended, the British reclaimed this institution, both the physical site and its symbolic value as a site of colonial knowledge production. The Raffles Library became Singapore's National Library in 1960, housing the country's government archives, and the building on Stamford Road houses today's National Museum of Singapore (Lee, 2016: 42)

***

At times, it was the most political of institutions that could remain the most intact. The wartime experience of the Philippines' commonwealth system illustrates how existing structures of government, personnel, and logics of operation established under Western rule could survive the Japanese occupation.

---

[64] On Koriba and other Japanese researchers such as the marine biologist Haneda Yata who was the Director of the Museum, see Arditti (1989) and Anctil (2018: 287–307). On the British side, Corner was joined by his former boss Richard Holttum, also a botanist and former Director of the Gardens and an ichthyologist named William Birtwhistle. *Malaya Tribune*, October 23, 1945; Anctil (2018: 294–299).

[65] Seet (1983) notes relatively minimal losses, whereas Lee (2016) estimates destruction on a greater scale, noting how "official papers of the Straits Settlements were thrown out and reportedly used in markets to wrap fish, meat and vegetables" (44).

[66] National Archives of Singapore, Oral History of Japanese Occupation of Singapore, Accession Number 000387, Tay Leong Hoe, Reel 2: 26.

First established in 1935, the Commonwealth system in the Philippines under the Americans encompassed a bundle of formal institutions for organizing political life in a tutelary fashion, which the colonizing power promised would end after a ten-year period and the Philippines would be granted full independence.[67] While the 1935 Commonwealth system included a Filipino chief executive, a popularly elected legislature, and a Supreme Court with a full-Filipino bench of justices, it was still a colonial democracy with a highly limited franchise in which less than 15 percent of the Philippine people were allowed to vote; and the Americans retained control over foreign policy, trade and defense. The commonwealth system also ushered in a new constitution that accorded strong coercive powers and fiscal prerogatives to the President.[68] The design of such representative institutions embedded many tensions, including an "overdeveloped" and unchecked executive branch capable of threatening to "emasculate the interests of the islands' dominant social class, an agro-commercial oligarchy entrenched in both houses of the national legislature" that also enjoyed muscular powers of policing, alongside a weakly centralized bureaucracy with limited territorial reach vis-à-vis provincial elites with strong political economic bases of power (Anderson, 1988; Hedman and Sidel, 2000: 15–16; McCoy, 2009).

During the occupation, the Japanese erred on the side of keeping, rather than overhauling, the formal political arena that the Americans had instituted. After Manila's takeover in January 1942, the residence of José Yulo – who would become Chief Justice of the Supreme Court during the occupation – bustled with meetings among prominent Filipino politicians who had remained in the city.[69] Maeda Masami, Chief of Staff to the 14th Army's Commander Homma Masaharu, had already reached out to Quintin Paredes (then Majority Floor Leader), Jorge Vargas (then Mayor of Manila), and (then Senators) Benigno Aquino and Claro Recto to compel their cooperation (Ikehata and Jose, 1999: 5–7). That substantive power would ultimately rest in the hands of the Japanese military authorities was a foregone conclusion, but these Filipino leaders still led a small group of elites that "grappled with the question of *how* they would

---

[67] On antecedent institutions for political representation in the Philippines under American rule, which include a bicameral legislature (1916) and municipal elections first held in 1901, see Anderson (1988) and Abinales and Amoroso (2017).

[68] Such executive authority included the ability to suspend habeas corpus in the face of "invasion, insurrection, or rebellion," centralized authority over both internal security and external defense forces, as well as "vast powers over matters of national finance and commerce as well as over government budget appropriations." McCoy (2009: 363) and Hedman and Sidel (2000: 15–16).

[69] Those who left Manila include the Commonwealth President Manuel Quezon who established a government-in-exile in Corregidor and later Washington D.C. On the different decisions of political elites as shaped by a variety of factors, including U.S. influence, Quezon's orders to Jose Vargas and others to remain in the city, as well as the individual sentiments and preoccupation ties with Japan, see Steinberg (1965, 1967), Rafael (1991), Ileto (2004), and Matthiessen (2016).

work with Japan" and deliberated possibilities, ranging from the creation of a new Philippine republic that would directly work with Homma's JMA to relatively lesser forms of collaboration by establishing a civil emergency administration or continuing the commonwealth with an elected president and vice president (Yellen, 2019: 118). What Maeda proffered in turn was a much narrower space for political maneuver, which gave the Philippine leaders only individual choices of whether or not to serve in a collaborationist government. Most chose the former, bringing into the Japanese-sponsored Second Philippine Republic's governing bodies, many of the same politicians who had occupied high positions in the American colonial commonwealth system.

Such continuity would color Manila's high politics throughout the Japanese occupation. Outside of the capital, and indeed, for much of the administrative, street-level governance of wartime Manila, much more change occurred. Especially during the last months of the war, scorched earth policies carried out by the soon-to-be-ousted Japanese and the artillery bombing of the returning Americans wrought terrible damage, reducing the city's infrastructure to rubble. Yet, alongside radical disruptions there was also striking persistence in the structure and workings of the legislature, executive, and courts as well as the people who ran them.[70] In June 1943, drafts for a new Philippine constitution were being drawn-up by a committee led by Laurel in his capacity as soon-to-be President of the Second Philippine Republic, which "used the 1935 charter [Philippine Constitution] as a template and made simple retouches – replacing the word 'Commonwealth' with 'Republic of the Philippines ... substituting 'ministers' for 'department secretaries'; and retaining practically the entire 'Bill of Rights,' but renaming it 'Duties and Rights of the Citizen'" (Ara, 2015: 178). In addition, the 1943 constitution of the Second Philippine Republic further strengthened the powers of the executive, which according to Shiba Minoru, the Japanese judicial advisor to the Philippine's JMA at the time, was because the "Japanese military authorities eagerly wanted to vest executive power on the president to facilitate the implementation of Japanese occupation policy" (Ara, 2015: 178). While some members of the drafting commission objected to the near-dictatorial nature of the executive branch and undemocratic nature of the government under the new constitution, the final version retained the preoccupation American blueprint for government with an emboldened role for the president.[71]

---

[70] Prior to October 1943, the Philippine Executive Commission under the 14th Army-led JMA had Vargas as its chairman with Aquino, Recto, Paredes as Commissioners of the interior; education, health and welfare; and public works and communications, respectively. The Second Philippine Republic continued along these lines with a cabinet "totally staffed and dominated by former Commonwealth officials of the highest rank," Goodman (1988: 101).

[71] For instance, Emilio Aguinaldo described how the "powers conferred upon the President are so absolute and illimitable that two influential persons may make arrangements to be elected

After the Japanese left, American colonial institutions for (limited) political representation, (diminished) democracy, and (imbalanced) separation of powers, carried over into the independent Philippines.[72] The enduring sinews of the 1935 commonwealth system and constitution ensured a strong executive office that undergirded the rise of presidential authoritarianism and patterns of political violence and bossism that would define Philippine politics into the second half of the twentieth century. The persistence of an overdeveloped executive branch further entrenched tensions between central and provincial authorities, while also aggravating the zero-sum nature of presidentialism and patronage-based electoral politics (Hutchcroft, 1988; Sidel, 1999; Quimpo, 2005).

3.2 What They Changed: Indirect Transmission

Many Western colonial institutions changed dramatically during the occupation. The experience of Burma's national military illustrates how an existing British colonial institution was substantively transformed under Japanese tutelage and indirectly transmitted into post-occupation Burma.

During the early twentieth century, the British in Burma had established a colonial army that relied mainly on soldiers from India and recruits among Karen, Chin, and Kachin groups from Burma's highland frontier areas.[73] Although the British in 1937 began to incorporate Burmese members from the country's lowland Irrawaddy Delta area, this ethnic majority group remained a quantitative minority within the colonial institution. The British Burma Army had narrow territorial reach beyond the capital of Rangoon, with practically no control over the countryside and limited channels for interacting with local populations. The British approach to organizing coercion in Burma at the time was to maintain a "skinny state" with limited contact with society and a colonial army with

---

alternatively to the position of President for six years each and continue in power thru the subsequent election of their descendants." See Ara (2015: 178–179).

[72] A striking pattern of individual-level continuity is the carryover of key personnel of the Second Philippine Republic's Ministry of Foreign Affairs into the Department of Foreign Affairs for the independent Philippines after 1946. For instance, Emilio Abello – the wartime Vice Minister of State for Foreign Affairs – became Minister Plenipotentiary to the United States in 1949; Salvador P. Lopez – the wartime press and publications officer – served as Undersecretary of foreign affairs and later the Philippines' ambassador to the United Nations, United States, and France; Jacinto C. Borja – the wartime Chief protocol officer – became Chief of the Division of European and African Affairs. See Yellen (2019: 202).

[73] The preoccupation British colonial army in today's Myanmar must be understood alongside the British Indian army and its deployment into Burma until 1937, when Burma was administratively separated from India. The British Burma Army was created in April 1, 1937. Seminal studies on the British colonial armed forces for Burma in this broader context include Callahan (2003), Taylor (2009). The systematic recruitment of ethnic minorities began after World War One, and while the British lifted a ban on Burmese enrollment in 1935, on the eve of the Japanese invasion, the ethnic composition of the British Burma Army was skewed in favor of indigenous groups vis-à-vis Burmese (Callahan, 2003: 33; Taylor, 2009: 100–101).

Rethinking Colonial Legacies across Southeast Asia   35

an imbalanced representation of ethnic groups in favor of the minority (Callahan, 2003: 22).

The Japanese did the opposite, giving official sanction to a Burmese-led armed force that reversed the ethnic imbalance. A key project along these lines was led by an organization with the Japanese army officer Suzuki Keiji at its helm called the Minami kikan, which according to Suzuki, was designed to "stir up disturbances throughout Burma in order to hamper the enemy's operations and to induce the Burmese to cooperate wholeheartedly with Japan."[74] Tasked in February 1940 by the IGH with collecting intelligence on ways to close down the Burma Road, Suzuki consolidated the material nucleus and initial membership of the Minami kikan, which included around twenty-five Japanese officers from the army and navy, as well as thirty Burmese nationalist elites seeking to fight for independence from the British (Yoon, 1978: 249–251).[75] The latter gained their first military training from Japanese instructors in mainland Japan, Hainan, and Taiwan, before eventually returning to what was still British-ruled Burma at the time. Led by Aung San, the "Thirty Comrades" or the Thakins, as they were associated with the Thakin Party, Dobama Asiayone, formally established the Burma Independence Army (BIA) in December 1941, which began with around two hundred Burmese recruits and would swiftly expand into a large-scale armed force throughout the country (Lebra, 1977: 62).[76]

Born as a Japanese-led volunteer army, the BIA evolved over the course of the occupation. A key promise that Suzuki had held out to the Thirty Comrades was that as soon as British rule in Burma was destroyed, the country would be fully independent, free of the Japanese as well. Initially, the hopeful BIA fought alongside the Japanese to first oust the British from the heartlands of Burma, and in the process, added more Burmese recruits, established a physical presence in territories beyond Rangoon in Central Burma and filled vacuums of lost British colonial governance with a decentralized system of administrative control, marking the first time in decades that "indigenous Burmans emerged as local state builders" (Callahan, 2003: 45).[77] During the spring of 1942, the BIA marched northward into Upper Burma and the frontier areas to further expel the British, as an enlarged force with a Burmese majority

---

[74] See Suzuki Keiji, "Plan for the Operation of Burma (Biruma Kōsaku Keikaku), December 1941 in Trager (1971: 27). Suzuki operated under the pseudonym Minami Masayo, taking "Minami," South, which "since he was assigned to Southeast Asia ... seemed an appropriate surname" and became the label for the kikan, organized under his purview. See Lebra (1977: 48).

[75] Lebra (1977), Taylor (2009), and Allen (2011).   [76] Maung Maung (1989) and Slater (2010).

[77] My summary of the BIA's evolution in this and the following paragraphs draws from Callahan (2003: 45–86). For an alternative reading of the BIA and its successors that sees the Japanese occupation as marking a greater disjuncture from the preoccupation colonial period, see Bayly and Harper (2007: 16–17, 60–75).

of soldiers with shared experiences that contributed to an emboldened sense of group solidarity. The Japanese helped reinforce such ethnicity-based identifications within this coercive institution by appointing Burmese staff officers, while also inculcating Japanese-style military training and discipline, for instance, through the introduction of a Soldier's Code in Japanese (Callahan, 2003: 55).

The BIA had many reincarnations. It became the Burma Defence Army (BDA) in July 1942. Fearing the BIA's growing influence in the countryside, the Japanese officially disbanded it and relaunched it under this new name. The restructured BDA further fanned nationalist sentiments premised upon being ethnic Burmese among its members, not least because they were small in number (which facilitated a cohesive military corporate identity); the Japanese introduced an Officer Training School (which created more shared experiences of arduous training and socialization); and the BDA was placed under the purview of a War Office (heavily staffed by Burmese officers). In 1943, the BDA was renamed the Burma National Army (BNA) and then the Patriotic Burmese Forces (PBF) in July 1945 (Callahan, 2003: 74 and 95).

The longer the Japanese remained in occupied Burma, the clearer the hollowness of past promises for true independence became to Burmese nationalist leaders. Disillusioned, many began to turn against the Japanese and aligned with the British, who had been seeking to reestablish a foothold in Upper Burma and were recruiting among Kachin, Karen, and other non-Burmese groups to mobilize anti-Japanese resistance.[78] In this process, a thorny question of how to manage the two groups within the same institution was resolved through a "Two Burma solution," which agreed to recruit soldiers throughout Burma (which the British favored because it could bring in their minority allies), but establishing separate wings for Burmese versus non-Burmese soldiers.[79] In making this possible, the institutional precedents of a "century-old British principle of colonial army organization: that of 'class' (i.e., ethnically

---

[78] In March 1945, the Burmese nationalists and BNA led by Aung San staged an uprising against the Japanese. The British Special Operations Executive (SOE) Force 136 played a central role organizing Kachin guerillas (around 16,000 men) and 2,000 Karen levies (around 12,000 men). See Callahan (2003: 71, 75–76, 80).

[79] At the helm of the BDA at the time, Aung San had favored a national army that kept a separate unit with Burmese officers, with soldiers recruited from the predominantly Burmese BDA/PDF. The British rejected this approach. Instead, Louis Mountbatten, the British Commander of SEAC offered a multi-ethnic army with two wings under a British Inspector General, with two separate Deputy Inspector Generals (DIG) – one Burmese DIG for ethnic Burmese soldiers and another Karen/Kachin/Chin DIG for non-Burmese soldiers. Striking a middle ground, the class battalion solution was preferred by Aung San. See Callahan (2003: 95). On divide-and-conquer, see Sadan (2013). For a remarkable portrayal of Aung San and his decisions in the broader context of Burmese anti-colonial national struggles and the occupation, see Naw (2001).

homogenous) battalions" were drawn upon (Callahan, 2003: 94–96). This arrangement was formalized between the British and Burmese in September 1945, as the Japanese occupation came to an end.

After the Japanese left, the British returned and stayed until 1948. The Two-Burma solution would undergird the national military of independent Burma, a coercive institution that blended together vestiges of the preoccupation British colonial army with wartime Japanese and Burmese-driven initiatives, as well as those of the post-occupation British. Although it appeared as a balanced multiethnic institution, the two-wing, separate class battalion arrangement was divisive.[80] And it soon became a source of explosive tensions both in the immediate wake of 1945 and for independent Burma in the form of civil war and separatist movements with enduring reifications of its ethnic and colonial origins, as well as the endurance of Burma's military authoritarian regime, the longest surviving of its kind during the twentieth century (Callahan, 2003; Turnell, 2011; Slater, Way, Lachapelle, and Casey, 2023).

***

Changes to Western colonial institutions were not limited to territories under direct Japanese military administration but also occurred where the Japanese formally recognized a foreign ruler's sovereignty. The experience of Indochina under joint Vichy French and Japanese rule illustrates how, within the wartime occupation milieu of the region, local agents of the non-Japanese empire could also substantively reconfigure preoccupation institutions.

The "Youth of the French Empire" was an umbrella organization for Indochina's many sports and scouting groups, charitable institutions and other initiatives for mobilizing youth, which was established in December 1941 (Raffin, 2005: 81).[81] At the time, the shadow of the Japanese imperial army loomed over the nominally French-ruled territory, under the purview of officers appointed by the Vichy-based fascist government of Philippe Pétain. Tasked with realizing Pétain's political vision of a National Revolution – which stridently advanced conservative values of "work, family, and fatherland" to replace the Third Republic's liberal, secular model of republicanism anchored in "freedom, equality, and fraternity" – Vichy officers stationed overseas in Indochina worked to translate and adapt metropolitan

---

[80] The Kandy Agreement dissatisfied both the Burmese majority (as it restricted the number of recruits and imposed ceilings on promotion) and the non-Burmese minority (as they sought better recognition and checks against the Burmese majority dominance). For instance, the Karens demanded an autonomous Karenistan with a territorial base, while the Chin Hills Battalion, which had longer precedents of serving with the prewar British colonial army, resented being treated as equals to Burmans with much shorter records of military service. See Callahan (2003: 99–106).

[81] On prior colonial institutions for youth and education in French Indochina under the Third Republic, see Brocheux and Hémery (2009) and Firpo (2016); on the role of the Catholic Church, see Keith (2012).

tenets to local political, cultural, and religious conditions, while also drawing upon and dramatically restructuring Indochina's pedagogical institutions (Marr, 1995; Grandjean, 2004; Jennings, 2011; Namba, 2012). To this end, the "Youth of the French Empire" served as a vehicle for inculcating new forms of patriotism, civic duty, and loyalty in the minds of the colonized through bodily discipline.

Stirring the hearts of colonized youth to serve an imperial nation was hardly a project unique to wartime Indochina.[82] What distinguished the Vichy French from the Third Republic was the former's explicitly state-directed approach to moral education that aimed to build a "three-layered patriotism": to France's empire transnationally, the federation of Indochina regionally, and locally, the five countries (pays) of Laos, Cambodia, and Annam, Tonkin, Cochinchina (the latter three of which comprise today's Vietnam) (Raffin, 2005: 5).

Oversight of this project fell under the purview of a General Commissariat for Physical Education, Sports, and Youth, a position first filled by the French Navy Captain Maurice Ducoroy. Ducoroy introduced sweeping changes to the organization of extracurricular activities and schooling across the colony (Ducoroy, 1949). Over 1,100 new stadiums were built, alongside an explosive growth in the number of sports leagues, scout groups, and local youth assemblies; Ducoroy took especial pride in organizing the first Tour d'Indochine cycling race, which traversed across all five parts of Indochina and he also "sponsored a big footrace from Phnom Penh to Hanoi, each part of the federation contributing one hundred relay runners" (Marr, 1995: 77–78). The Vichy trained new teachers for classrooms with revised curricula that prioritized physical exercise, hygiene, handicrafts, and choral singing. Such projects aimed at depoliticizing colonized subjects while countering the appeal of the Japanese, not least for fears that their rallying call for pan-Asian solidarity would spur anti-French resistance in Indochina (Marr, 1995: 76–77). "In the context of the urgent necessity to distract the Indochinese from the Japanese 'hype' and knowing the extraordinary taste of Orientals for big festivals," explained one Vichy administrator in Vietnam at the time, "I have sponsored sporting events on a federal scale which for months have occupied minds and have found considerable success with millions of enthusiastic and sometimes excited spectators" (Raffin, 2005: 78). In turn, locally stationed Japanese civilian and military personnel also organized "projects designed to convince Indochinese of Japanese superiority and the longer-term merits of participation in the Greater East Asia Co-Prosperity Sphere" and after the March 1945 coup, the new Japanese Governor's assistant Iida was tasked with converting the infrastructures that

---

[82] For instance, see Chatani (2018) on Japanese efforts to mobilize agrarian youth in occupied Southeast Asia as extended from earlier colonies of Korea and Taiwan that in turn, mimicked Japan's village youth associations (2–3).

Ducoroy had established into a paramilitary Vanguard Youth organization (Marr, 1995: 81 and 133–136, quote from 81).

Local adaptations emerged. Compared with Vietnam where youth corps were organized centrally and trained under the watchful eye of authorities like Ducoroy, Cambodia's youth corps and scout movements were organized more indirectly under the purview of King Sihanouk, who fostered a royalist form of local nationalism that appealed to people's allegiance toward the monarchy through activities that "promoted Angkor and the Khmer kings of yore as the embodiment of Cambodge's past grandeur and future promise" (Edwards, 2007: 232). In Laos, the Lao Nhay movement – created in 1941 under the direction of Charles Rochet, the director of public education for Laos – did not directly mobilize youth through new organizations, but rather focused on cultural, identity building activities, "language formation, redefined political borders, and emotional appeals through songs and hero glorification." (Rochet, 1946; Raffin, 2005: 133–141, quote from 135). Sports leagues and youth organizations were relatively weaker in Laos, where Rochet focused more attention to restoring monuments and organizing festivals.

Religion played a central role in wartime youth mobilization projects. Agents of both France's wartime empire and that of Japan favored religions that were seen as embracing hierarchical views of society that could generate obedience and submissiveness to state authority.[83] Ducoroy's office ordered the restoration of the temples of Confucius in Vietnam and revived the festival of Van-Thanh, while in Cambodia, the Buddhist Institute in Phnom Penh became a busy site for state-sponsored religious festivals (Keyes, 1994: 47–51). The Japanese adopted similar approaches to harnessing the appeal of indigenous religions that they perceived as sources of authentic values in Indochina (Werner, 1981; Tran, 1996). For instance, the Japanese built ties with leaders of the Cao Dai Church, a syncretic religion strong in southern Vietnam that blended precepts and practices from Buddhism, Confucianism, Taoism, and Christianity, while Cao Dai workers and youth received basic military training from IJN personnel (Marr 1995, 83–84).

Well after the occupation ended, projects for mobilizing youth and religion in Indochina under Vichy French and Japanese rule would continue to influence the colony's long road to independence from the returning French as well as postcolonial nation-building endeavors. In Vietnam, wartime schools for youth cadres and instructors strengthened the Viet Minh during the First Indochina War (1946–1954) by supplying manpower and organizational tactics as well as

---

[83] For a lucid examination of Vichy efforts to coopt Buddhist associations in Cambodia as well as the broader cultural and domestic political milieu in which it occurred, see Edwards (2007: 233–240) and Gunn (2012: 11–18). For an equally excellent account of Laos, see Ivarsson (1999).

a leadership with shared training experience in Vichy-sponsored youth corps.[84] After independence, Ngo Dinh Diem, the first president of the Republic of Vietnam (South Vietnam) initially revived Ducoroy's approach to centralizing control over youth corps, scout movements and recreational activities, while espousing a vision of a National Revolution reminiscent of Pétain's in ways that summoned civic duty, sacrifice, and public service ethos.[85] In Cambodia, King Sihanouk would build the Royal Khmer Socialist Youth, which "bore the legacy of the Vichy youth initiative," while in Laos, wartime institutions for mobilizing youth and religion were instrumentalized by competing forces seeking to politicize the Sangha monks to advance their political causes (Raffin, 2005: 219).[86] The wartime institutions that at once drew upon and reconfigured the French colonial past would leave uneven and lasting imprints.

3.3 What They Created: Non-Transmission

The Japanese occupation was a time of dark creativity during which deeply troubling yet innovative solutions to problems of military governance were introduced across Southeast Asia. Territories once formally divided under multiple Western powers became interconnected through projects for organizing the movement of people under a single Japanese empire.

Against the backdrop of European and American colonial rule, new institutions emerged for transferring men and women to places of Japanese military need across Southeast Asia. The rōmusha, a category of coerced and quasi-coerced laborers, were tasked with manual work building infrastructures for wartime defense and transportation. Although deeply exploitative labor regimes in the service of American, British, Dutch, French, and Portuguese colonial interests were already a preoccupation fixture throughout Southeast Asia, what the Japanese introduced anew was a form of centrally coordinated transnational

---

[84] Writing in 1946, Paul Mus would discern that anti-French resistance in Vietnam had an underlying structure, driven by the "vanguard youth" that Ducoroy had organized. See Mus (1946: 451). On individual-level linkages between Vichy and Japanese youth organization and the Viet Minh, see Marr (1995: 214–225) and Raffin (2005: 195–197). This is but one strand within the complex legacies of the Japanese occupation for the strength of the Vietnam nationalist movement, which have been the subject of rich scholarship. See Marr (1995, 2013), Vu (2014), and Lentz (2019).

[85] Ngo Dinh Diem would soon abandon the Vichy rhetoric and fashion a political ideology of Personalism but with significant continuities in terms of techniques for organizing youth corps and Vichyist ceremonies. See Raffin (2005: 200–217). For illuminating histories of the broader context of Diem's political ideology and postcolonial Vietnam's nation-state building from a transnational perspective, see Bradley (2000) and Nguyen (2017).

[86] For details on cross-country differences, see invaluable works by Raffin (2002, 2005), which draw connections between subnational variations to wartime youth mobilization within Indochina to the relative strength of political leadership and anti-colonial resistance across Vietnam, Laos, and Cambodia as well as the nature of their postcolonial authoritarian regimes.

Rethinking Colonial Legacies across Southeast Asia 41

mobility.[87] For instance, between September 1942 and October 1943, the Japanese sent approximately 90,000 rōmusha from Burma and 78,000 from Malaya, and smaller numbers of laborers from Java and Indochina to help build the Siam-Burma "Death" Railway – 400 km of train tracks and 600 bridges, connecting Rangoon to Bangkok – that enabled the IJA to send weapons and manpower to fight land campaigns against the Allied forces (Nakahara, 2015: 252; Melber, 2016: 169–170). New transnational mobilities also defined the heiho, a category of auxiliary soldiers created by the Japanese.[88] A man from Malaya, summoned to serve as a heiho, found himself first plunged into the depths of the Malay jungles (where he was tasked with "cleaning up" after the 16th Army's attacks on British soldiers and Chinese communists) and then sent to Burma (where he helped dig trenches for the Victoria airfield and managed paperwork for people crossing the border with Thailand, stamping their forms).[89]

Transnational arrangements for satisfying the labor appetites of the IJA also included those exploiting and enslaving women for sexual labor. The Japanese wartime empire's system of "institutionalized rape," euphemistically called the comfort women system, linked Southeast Asia to East Asia through the forced transfer of women from earlier occupied parts of the Japanese empire to military brothels in Southeast Asia for purposes of sexual slavery.[90] As early as February 1942, the Southern Army General Command asked the Taiwan Army to "dispatch as soon as possible fifty native comfort women to Borneo" (Nakahara, 2001: 583); women from Taiwan as well as Korea and China entered so-called comfort stations throughout today's Brunei, Sarawak, and Malaysia serving officers, soldiers, guards, and staff at Japanese army garrisons and internment

---

[87] Across Burma, Java, Sumatra, and the Malay peninsula, the Japanese term romusha replaced the English word coolie (or Dutch koelie) for unskilled laborers who worked temporary jobs in physically arduous conditions. Romusha has often been used in reference to forced laborers recruited from Java but recent scholarship shows that it was an empire-wide term. Java is conventionally understood as the largest site of recruitment with an estimated 4 million romusha, among which nearly 300,000 Javanese were sent overseas, compared with approximately 1.2 million from all other Southeast Asian territories under Japanese occupation. See de Jong (2002: 242–251), Hovinga (2005: 214–215), Melber (2016: 169–170), and Huff (2020: 46).

[88] Maekawa (2002: 185–189) identifies three distinct stages for heiho recruitment in Java and the Outer Islands, from prisoners of war with military experience, to unemployed young men without military experience (after May 1943), to large-scale forced recruitment (after March 1944), and during a final stage of mid-1944 onwards, trained at the Naval Heiho Training School.

[89] National Archives of Singapore, Oral History of Japanese Occupation of Singapore, Accession Number 000498, Alias bin Osman, Disc 6, 52–54; Disc 9, 76–79.

[90] During the first year of Southeast Asia's large-scale invasion, a report in September 1942 from the Ministry of the Army noted that "comfort facilities ... have been set up total 100 in North China, 140 in Central China, 40 in South China, 100 in South East Asia (Nanpo), 10 in the Southern Seas (Nankai) and 10 in Sakhalin, for a grand total of 400." See Hirofumi (1998: 212). See Morris-Suzuki (2015: 6–10) for a nuanced discussion of controversies relating to the terms of forced transportation [kyōsei renkō] or sexual slavery [sei doreisei].

camps.[91] Korean "comfort women" were found in Burma – from the outskirts of Rangoon to the oil refining town of Syriam (today's Thanlyin) – as well as in Thailand and Singapore (Morris-Suzuki, 2015: 3 and 7). While it is difficult to ascertain the total number of women recruited and transferred throughout the occupation period, historians exploring available records and oral testimonies recognize "the huge geographical extent of the 'comfort station' network and of the vast distances over which many women were transported" (Morris-Suzuki, 2015: 5). Such trans-regional flows of forced female sexual labor went alongside the movement of Southeast Asian "comfort women" within the region: notable but hardly exclusive flows included women moving from Malaysia to Thailand and Burma – as Nakahara Michiko's powerful essay illustrates through the figure Ms. X, a Muslim Malay woman "who was taken with her husband to a construction site of the Burma-Siam Railway ... [and was] used as a sex slave in the camp" – and from Java to Borneo and East Timor.[92] While military brothels had been familiar establishments in Southeast Asia under European and American colonial rule, the Japanese occupation ushered in novel forms of centrally coordinated pan-Asian connectivity.

Money also knitted together Southeast and East Asia together in unprecedented ways. The Japanese issued military currencies throughout occupied territories, endeavoring to build a quasi-yen bloc in Southeast Asia, which drew upon precedents from occupied China (Nakamura, 1996: 185). Into 1942, nearly all European banks across Southeast Asia were shut down and the Japanese sought to integrate hitherto separate monetary systems across the region.[93] Scrip was issued initially by the military and eventually by the Southern Regions Development Bank, which along with the Yokohama Specie Bank and the Bank of Taiwan, served as Tokyo's key vehicle for centralizing control over banking throughout occupied territories (Huff, 2020a: 86–88). Banana plants adorned the notes for Malaya and Indonesia; pagodas were drawn on Burmese notes, which the Japanese referred to as kyat, a reference to the "old Burmese name for the silver coins issued by King Mindon ... of course, the name was deliberately employed to make the new 'currency' more acceptable, and a gesture to the fiction that the Japanese had arrived as liberators from colonialism" (Turnell and Bradford, 2009: 5).

Many institutions for colonial military governance across occupied Southeast Asia were learned not only from territories under Japanese rule, but also other

---

[91] Ooi (2011: 68), Table 6.3.   [92] Nakahara (2001: 585). See also Ooi (2011: 66–68).
[93] For details on wartime efforts to build central banks and complexities of financial institutions in various occupied territories, see Takagi (2016: 69–73), Saito (2017), Kratoska (2018: 219–227), and Huff (2020: 84–102). For an especially vivid account of the workings of Japanese military currency and its lasting socio-legal impact in Burma and Malaya, see Ramnath (2023).

Axis-aligned countries or metropolitan Japan. For instance, in Java and the Philippines, Nazi Germany's Propaganda Korps served as a model for ordering cultural life. During a tour of Europe in 1940, Yamashita Tomoyuki had admired what he saw as effective ways of winning the hearts-and-minds of people through the uses of art, music, and widespread dissemination of information (Mark, 2014: 1184). At the time, the IJA was already confronting the limitations of its propaganda scheme in China, which relied on an internal Broadcast and Pacification Unit with limited public reach.[94] Ethan Mark's (2014) penetrating study of the Java Propaganda Squad shows how writers, artists, filmmakers, musicians, dramatists from Japan were recruited to design a culture for mass consumption aimed at summoning the patriotic passions of the Indonesian people. In the Philippines, the propaganda squad similarly brought in a diverse group of civilians to tame popular sentiment in ways adapted to local conditions.[95] Radio broadcasts of Domei-dispatched news in English, Tagalog, Spanish, Japanese, and later in Visayan were made (Terami-Wada, 1990: 289). Projects aimed at persuading enemy soldiers to surrender also emerged, with the propaganda squad issuing leaflets denouncing racial discrimination by Americans against Filipino men in uniform, stoking national pride and memories of the Philippine Revolution, appealing to sentimental and sexual desires, nostalgia, as well as by issuing so-called armistice tickets and organizing "good will" missions to assure people in the provinces of normalcy in the capital (Terami-Wada, 1990: 292–299).

Imported from metropolitan Japan, neighborhood associations called tonarigumi became a fresh fixture in many parts of Southeast Asia.[96] As a state-directed institution for clustering ten to fifteen households into a collective unit, the Japanese government had used tonarigumi during the late 1930s to mobilize manpower among its own citizens and organize local defenses against air raids as well as to improve the efficiency of supplying materials to the government and distributing controlled goods. As the empire expanded, this metropolitan institution was extended to Southeast Asia; under the oversight of JMA administrators, members of each collective unit shared responsibility for recruiting labor, collecting foodstuff and war materials as well as mutual surveillance of neighbors.

The role of on-site officers of the Japanese imperial military establishment as conduits for the local adaptation of borrowed foreign or metropolitan Japanese institutions is well-illustrated by agricultural settlements in today's Malaysia. In

---

[94] Terami-Wada (1990: 280–281) and Mark (2014: 1184–1185).
[95] Its membership included "six novelists and poets, four painters, nine newspaper and magazine workers, five cameramen, two broadcasting technicians, four printing technicians, fourteen Catholic priests, twelve Protestant ministers, and five movie people," along with a hundred correspondents from Japanese newspaper companies. See Terami-Wada (1990: 283).
[96] Kurasawa (1988). For an excellent analysis of the legacies of the tonarigumi for the postindependence Indonesian state, see Jaffrey (2019: 122–137).

1943, the Japanese relocated at least 300,000 people from Singapore to rural areas in the Malay peninsula in order to build enclaves for self-sufficient food production. This official project was part of a larger initiative to restructure the Malayan economy amidst wartime exigencies. Inflation was rising; the Allied forces were planning a blockade, which would only worsen an already dire food shortage. Politically as well, it made sense from the Japanese perspective to "remov[e] local residents (with their suspect loyalties) to sites that were unlikely to become major battlefields."[97] There were many agricultural settlements, divided generally along ethnic lines. For instance, the Chinese would move to Endau in Johor (called New Syonan), the Eurasians to Bahau in Negeri Sembilan (called Fuji-go, or Fuji village), and the Malays and Indians to the Riau Islands.[98]

A Japanese officer named Shinozaki Mamoru, with the Welfare Department of the Singapore Municipal Administration, was central to the design of such institutions. His orders came from higher authorities in the IJA's headquarters that ordered local officials in Japanese-occupied Singapore to stabilize the colony. In turn, according to Shinozaki, "[t]he new mayor [of Singapore] placed the burden of the evacuation squarely on my shoulders. 'You organize it,' he said" (Shinozaki, 1975: 80). Shinozaki had certain precedents in mind. Wartime evacuations of city populations in Tokyo to live with up-country relatives were already ongoing in Japan; and he was familiar with "the story of how Marshal Balboa of Italy had forced Italians to emigrate to the Libyan desert before World War Two" (Shinozaki, 1975: 80).

However, occupied Syonan was neither Tokyo nor Italy. "My job," recalled Shinozaki, was "to force thousands of Syonans to emigrate to Malaya immediately," unlike the Italian evacuation, which had taken two years. Also, most residents of occupied Singapore did not have kinship ties outside of the city (unlike those in Tokyo). The solution, he decided, was to work through local elites. Shinozaki summoned well-respected leaders from the major ethnic communities to serve as liaisons and create quasi-official organizations, such as the Overseas Chinese Association (OCA) and Eurasian Welfare Association (created in 1942) (Shinozaki, 1975: 64).

Endau hosted the largest settlement, large stretches of land carved out of the deep jungle in the shape of a giant bowl (Shinozaki, 1975: 85). It received a first wave of 200 Chinese settlers on December 21, 1943 who began cultivating

---

[97] Eaton (2014: 47).
[98] There were at least thirty resettlement schemes for the Chinese population, most of which were aimed at food production, but at least three also involved resettling people suspected of supporting communist guerillas. See Kratoska (2018: 281). Here, I focus on Endau. On the Eurasian Bahua settlement, see Hodgkins (2014). For an excellent comparison of the two agricultural settlements, see Eaton (2018: 257–270).

Formosan rice and table vegetables. By the end of 1944, the recorded number of inhabitants rose to 12,000 (Shinozaki, 1975: 85). The Japanese treated Endau as an autonomous zone under OCA leadership, which included the influential Straits Chinese leader Lim Boon Keng, that oversaw local administration, policing, and fundraising to sustain the settlement.[99] Swiftly, the Chinese-run enclave gained a tool shop, a paper factory, a sawmill, a school, a bank, barbers, pawnshops, pharmacies, restaurants and hotels, as well as streets with bright gas lights. Entertainment was spare, recalled one former resident, "unless there [was] a special day like for instance, Chinese New Year; they would bring the Chinese *wayang* [theatre performance] over, Chinese *wayang* from Singapore … on [a] special day like Emperor's birthday, a film unit did come out from Singapore to show propaganda films. They put a truck and they got a school hall, they rent the school hall to show the films from 8.00 [pm] to 11.00 pm, and one Chinese film."[100] The transient economic and social life of Endau settlement ended as a failed project of wartime management. Rice production never reached levels of self-sufficiency, not least because few settlers knew how to grow rice and everyday social order broke down due to attacks from anti-Japanese resistance forces, most often members of the MPAJA (Malayan Peoples' Anti-Japanese Army). When the Japanese left, Endau Settlement's infrastructures were abandoned, just as quickly as they had been erected.[101]

4 Conclusion

During the nineteenth and first half of the twentieth centuries, Southeast Asia was colonized by multiple foreign powers. Prevailing scholarship on long-run colonial legacies tends to focus on the enduring influence of institutions introduced under European and American empires over today's politics, economies, and society. However, the Japanese empire's occupation of the region from 1940 to 1945 during World War Two complicates any narrative that presumes

---

[99] There are competing interpretations of the relationship between Shinozaki and Lim Boon Keng, ranging from Shinozaki's self-congratulatory account of how he had helped secure Lim's released from the Kempeitai and the latter's willingness to serve on a "New Syonan Model Farm Construction Committee" and active involvement in joining Shinozaki's team of surveyors to identify suitable agricultural settlement sites (Turnbull, 1989: 195) to more measured accounts of Lim's reluctant cooperation (Huang, 2020: 6). I am grateful to Tiffany Tam for this reading.

[100] National Archives of Singapore, Oral History of Japanese Occupation of Singapore, Accession No. 000535, Wan Leong Gay 1985, Disc 4, 52–55. On Endau's formal autonomy from Japanese law, but also, its surveillance through informants, see Kratoska (2018: 281).

[101] The afterlives of Endau Settlement into post-occupation Malaya were multiple. Cheah (2012) argues that it became used as a base for communist guerilas and helped lay the foundations for the "Chinese squatter problem" outside of urban areas during the Malayan Emergency (38). According to Shinozaki himself, who returned to Malaysia in the mid-1970s, Endau had become a watermelon growing center (Shinozaki, 1975: 86).

historical persistence. This Element has offered a framework for analyzing this period as a critical juncture during which varieties of projects for wartime governance under Japanese military rule operated and selectively carried over the region's Western colonial institutions through the war. It has explored three types of processes – direct transmission, indirect transmission, and new creation – through which existing arrangements were either kept or changed, or unprecedented ones emerged during the occupation. While such processes of institutional interaction (or lack thereof) were highly context-dependent, a pivotal set of actors for understanding how and why they varied are the military officers and civilian agents of wartime empires stationed overseas who exercised situational autonomy over local governance.

This Element's approach to rethinking colonial legacies across Southeast Asia, through the lens of the Japanese wartime empire, provides several future directions for research. First, it gives reason for scholars to grapple with transnational connections when studying the long-run consequences of colonial institutions. The Japanese occupation of Southeast Asia involved extensive sharing and learning of institutional templates from earlier conquered territories, especially in China, Korea, and Taiwan. The workings of even the most seemingly local of institutions, from the remote jungles of Malaysia to the urban heart of Manila, were inextricably tied to Japan's ambitions and anxieties for managing its overseas empire. Southeast Asia also became more tightly connected to East Asia and the Pacific Islands through the transfer of labor, forced mobilities, as well as economic crises and ideological claims that densely wove together colonies once divided under multiple Western imperial powers.

Second, during the occupation, Southeast Asia's colonial territorial borders and administrative boundaries shifted in certain places, and the sizes and shapes of countries changed temporarily. For instance, Thailand grew larger while today's Cambodia, Malaysia, and Myanmar became smaller. Today's Indonesia was split as the Japanese military administered the island of Sumatra as part of Malaya until 1943. After 1945, some preoccupation borders were restored, a process that was uncontroversial in certain sites but would stoke loud claims to irredentism and conflicts in other places. The shifting political geography of Southeast Asia, as such, is important to understand, not least because post-occupation reversions may make it seem as if there was more stability to territorial and administrative boundaries over time than was actually the case.

Third, the Japanese occupation commands attention to issues of race and ethnicity in ways that bring intra-Asian divides to the forefront when studying colonial legacies across Southeast Asia. Japan's imperial identity as a self-avowed Asian empire complicated us-them binaries of European (and American) versus Asian, white versus non-white that had hitherto separated colonizer versus colonized, while also blurring many identity categories that had undergirded Western institutions for divide-and-conquer and the colonial politics of difference more generally. On the one hand, the Japanese wartime empire's visions of a Greater East Asia Co-Prosperity Sphere and ways of appealing to co-ethnic, shared racial ties generated new forms of pan-Asian identification and bolstered felt imperatives for solidarity. On the other hand, Japan's imperial ideologies advanced the superiority of the Yamato race of Japan as a master people over other Asians, while also fostering racialized hierarchies among Southeast Asian populations and giving greater salience to ethnicized differences and communal rivalries, not least by introducing reversals of fortune between minority ethnic groups (that the Western colonial powers had favored) and majority groups (with grievances that the Japanese colonial power appealed to). Coprosperity was not equality. At a time when the Western colonial powers receded briefly from the main frame of politics, social categories and group boundaries became malleable and were often drawn in contra-distinction to other Asians.

Finally, this Element generates opportunities to further enrich social scientific inquiries into the mechanisms through which colonial institutions have lasting impacts on contemporary outcomes in Southeast Asia. Taking seriously the potentially mediating role of the Japanese occupation and specifying different processes of transmission opens avenues for parsing out whether, and to what extent, features of post-independence states, societies, and economies are attributable to Western versus Japanese colonial institutions, as well as for distinguishing between the effects of war and the effects of colonial institutions. Moving beyond the formal institutions examined here, scholars may also gain reason to be more curious about the varieties of informal and illicit institutions that sustained the Japanese wartime empire in Southeast Asia. And by way of gaining a fuller picture of the messily complicated nature of institutional life during tragic times of war, scholars may also struggle productively with balancing a need for a tamable past in order to tell causal stories about colonial legacies with keen appreciation for the complexities of historical experience, lived and remembered.

References

Abinales, P. (1997). Davao-kuo: The Political Economy of a Japanese Settler Zone in Philippine Colonial Society. *Journal of American-East Asian Relations*, 6(1), 59–82.

(2003). Progressive-Machine Conflict in Early Twentieth-Century U.S. Politics and Colonial-State Building in the Philippines. In Go, J. and Foster, A. (eds.) *The American Colonial State in the Philippines: Global Perspectives*. Durham, NC: Duke University Press, pp. 148–181.

Abinales, P. and Amoroso, D. (2017). *State and Society in the Philippines*. Lanham, MD: Rowman & Littlefield.

Adams, J. (1996). Principals and Agents, Colonialists and Company Men: The Decay of Colonial Control in the Dutch East Indies. *American Sociological Review*, 61(1), 12–28.

Agoncillo, T. (1965). *The Fateful Years: Japan's Adventure in the Philippines, 1941–1945*. Quezon City: Garcia.

Akashi, Y. (1970). Japanese Policy towards the Malayan Chinese 1941–1945. *Journal of Southeast Asian Studies*, 1(2), 61–89.

(2008a). Japanese Research Activities in Occupied Malaya/Syonan. In Akashi, Y. and Yoshimura, M. (eds.) *New Perspectives of the Japanese Occupation of Malaya and Singapore, 1941–1945*. Singapore: National University of Singapore Press, pp. 158–185.

(2008b). An Annotated Bibliographical Study of the Japanese Occupation of Malaya/Singapore, 1941–45. In Akashi, Y. and Yoshimura, M. (eds.) *New Perspectives of the Japanese Occupation of Malaya and Singapore, 1941–1945*. Singapore: National University of Singapore Press, pp. 250–284.

Akashi, Y. and Yoshimura, M. (eds.). (2008). *New Perspectives of the Japanese Occupation of Malaya and Singapore, 1941–1945*. Singapore: National University of Singapore Press.

Akira, I. (1965). *After Imperialism: The Search for a New Order in the Far East, 1921–1931*. Cambridge, MA: Harvard University Press.

Allen, L. (2011). Fujiwara and Suzuki: The Lawrence of Arabia Syndrome. In Nish, I. and Allen, M. (eds.) *War, Security, and Conflict in Japan and the Asia Pacific, 1941–1952: The Writings of Louis Allen*. Vol. 4. Folkestone, UK: Global Oriental, pp. 267–276.

Amrith, S. (2013). *Crossing the Bay of Bengal: The Furies of Nature and the Fortunes of Migrants*. Cambridge, MA: Harvard University Press.

References

Amrith, S. and Harper, T. (2014). Introduction. In Amrith, S. and Harper T. (eds.) *Histories of Health in Southeast Asia: Perspectives on the Long Twentieth Century*. Bloomington, IN: Indiana University Press, pp. 1–16.

Anamwathana, P. (2020). *Thailand during World War Two: Impact and Aftermath*. PhD Thesis. Oxford, UK: Oxford University.

Anderson, B. (1988). Cacique Democracy and the Philippines: Origins and Dreams. *New Left Review*, 169: 3–31

Anderson, B. (2006). *Java in a Time of Revolution: Occupation and Resistance, 1944–1946*. Jakarta: PT Equinox Publishing Indonesia.

Anctil, M. (2018). *Luminous Creatures: The History and Science of Light Production in Living Organisms*. Montreal: McGill-Queen's University Press.

Ara, S. (2015). Emilio Aguinaldo under American and Japanese Rule Submission for Independence? *Philippine Studies: Historical & Ethnographic Viewpoints*, 63(2), 161–192.

Arditti, J. (1989). Kwan Koriba: Botanist and Soldier. *Garden's Bulletin, Singapore*, 42(1), 1–17.

Aso, M. (2013). Patriotic Hygiene: Tracing New Places of Knowledge Production about Malaria in Vietnam, 1919–75. *Journal of Southeast Asian Studies*, 44(3), 423–443.

(2018). *Rubber and the Making of Vietnam: An Ecological History, 1897–1975*. Chapel Hill, NC: University of North Carolina Press.

Aung-Thwin, M. (2005). Colonialism: Southeast Asia. In Horowitz, M. C. (ed.) *New Dictionary in the History of Ideas*, Vol. 1. Detroit: Charles' Scribner's Sons, pp. 377–381.

Aydin, C. (2007). *The Politics of Anti-westernism in Asia: Visions of World Order in Pan-Islamic and Pan-Asian Thought*. New York, NY: Columbia University Press.

Bayly, C. and Harper, T. (2005). *Forgotten Armies: The Fall of British Asia, 1941–1945*. Cambridge, MA: Harvard University Press.

(2007). *Forgotten Wars: Freedom and Revolution in Southeast Asia*. Cambridge, MA: Harvard University Press.

Benda, H. (1958). *The Crescent and the Rising Sun: Indonesian Islam under the Japanese Occupation, 1942–1945*. The Hague: W. Van Hoeve.

(1972). *Continuity and Change in Southeast Asia*. New Haven, CT: Yale University Southeast Asia Studies.

Benda, H., Irikura, J., and Kishi, K. (eds.). (1965). *Japanese Military Administration in Indonesia: Selected Documents*. Translated from Japanese by J. Irikura, M. Broekhuysen, & I. Pamoedjo. New Haven, CT: Yale University Southeast Asia Series.

Bertrand, J. and Laliberté, A. (eds.). (2010). *Multination States in Asia: Accommodation or Resistance*. New York, NY: Cambridge University Press.

Blackburn, K. (2019). Recalling War Trauma of the Pacific War and the Japanese Occupation in the Oral History of Malaysia and Singapore. *Oral History Review*, 36(2), 231–252.

Blaydes, L. and Gryzmala-Busse, A. (2023). Historical State Formation within and beyond Europe. *World Politics*, 75(5), 1–18.

Booth, A. (2007). *Colonial Legacies: Economic and Social Development in East and Southeast Asia*. Honolulu, HI: University of Hawai'i Press.

Booth, A. and Deng, K. (2017). Japanese Colonialism in Comparative Perspective. *Journal of World History*, 28(1), 61–98.

Bowie, K. (2010). Women's Suffrage in Thailand: A Southeast Asian Historiographical Challenge. *Comparative Studies in Society and History*, 52(4), 708–741.

Bradley, M. (2000). *Imagining Vietnam and America: The Making of Postcolonial Vietnam, 1919–1950*. Chapel Hill, NC: University of North Carolina Press.

Bradsher, G. (2006). *Japanese War Crimes and Related Topics: A Guide to Records at the National Archives*. Washington DC: U.S. National Archives and Records Service.

Brocheux, P. (2009). *Une histoire économique du Viet Nam: 1850–2007: la planache et al camion*. Paris: Les Indes savantes.

Brocheux, P. and Hémery, D. (2009). *Indochina: An Ambiguous Colonization, 1858–1954*. Berkeley, CA: University of California Press.

Brook, T. (2012). Hesitating Before the Judgment of History. *Journal of Asian Studies*, 71(1): 103–114.

Brown, I. (2011). Tracing Burma's Economic Failure to Its Colonial Inheritance. *Business History Review*, 85(4), 725–747.

Bunzl, M. (2004). Counterfactual History: A User's Guide. *American Historical Review*, 109(3), 845–858.

Callahan, M. (2003). *Making Enemies: War and State Building in Burma*. Ithaca, NY: Cornell University Press.

Charoenvattananukul, P. (2020). *Ontological Security and Status Seeking: Thailand's Provocative Behaviours during the Second World War*. Abingdon: Routledge.

Clulow, A. (2013). Like Lambs in Japan and Devils Outside Their Land: Diplomacy, Violence, and Japanese Merchants in Southeast Asia. *Journal of World History*, 24(2), 335–358.

Conrad, S. (2014). The Dialectics of Remembrance: Memories of Empire in Cold War Japan. *Comparative Studies in Society and History*, 56(1), 4–33.

Capoccia, G. and Kelemen, D. (2007). The Study of Critical Junctures: Theory, Narrative, and Counterfactuals in Historical Institutionalism. *World Politics*, 59(3), 341–369.

Chakrabarty, D., Harrison, R., and Jackson, P. (2018) (eds.) *The Ambiguous Allure of the West: Traces of the Colonial in Thailand*. Ithaca, NY: Cornell University Press.

Chatani, S. (2018). *Nation-Empire: Ideology and Rural Youth Mobilization in Japan and Its Colonies*. Ithaca, NY: Cornell University Press.

Charney, M. and Naono, A. (2015). The Burmese Economy under the Japanese Occupation, 1942–1945. In Boldorf, M. & Okazaki, T. (eds.) *Economies under Occupation: The Hegemony of Nazi Germany and Imperial Japan in World War II*. Abingdon: Routledge, 218–231.

Cheah, B. K. (1988). The Erosion of Ideological Hegemony and Royal Power and the Rise of Postwar Malay Nationalism, 1945–46. *Journal of Southeast Asian Studies*, 19(1): 1–26.

(2012). *Red Star over Malaya: Resistance and Social Conflict during and after the Japanese Occupation of Malaya, 1941–46*. 4th ed. Singapore: National University of Singapore Press.

Cheesman, N. (2016). Rule-of-Law Lineages in Colonial and Early Post-Colonial Burma. *Modern Asian Studies*, 50(2): 564–601.

(2017). How in Myanmar "National Races" Came to Surpass Citizenship and Exclude Rohingya. *Journal of Contemporary Asia*, 47(3), 461–483.

Chua, B. H. (2003). Multiculturalism in Singapore: An Instrument of Social Control. *Race & Class*, 44(3): 58–77

Cirone, A. and Pepinsky, T. (2022). Historical Persistence. *Annual Review of Political Science*, 25, 241–259.

Clancey, G. (2002). The Japanese Imperium and South-East Asia: An Overview. In Kratoska, P. (ed.) *Southeast Asian Minorities in the Wartime Japanese Empire*. Abingdon: RoutledgeCurzon, pp. 7–20.

Collier, D. (2011). Understanding Process Tracing. *PS: Political Science & Politics*, 44(4): 823–830

Coox, A. (1985). *Nomonhan: Japan against Russia, 1939*. Stanford, CA: Stanford University Press.

Corner, E. J. H. (1981). *The Marquis: A Tale of Syonan-to*. Singapore: Heinemann Asia.

CuUnjieng, N. (2017). Cultures of Empire, Nation, and Universe in Pres. José P. Laurel's Political Thought, 1927–1949. *Philippines Studies: Historical and Ethnographic Viewpoints*, 65(1), 3–30.

Cyr, J. and Goodman, S. (2024) (eds.). *Doing Good Qualitative Research*. New York: Oxford University Press.

De Juan, A. and Pierskalla, J. H. (2017). The Comparative Politics of Colonialism and Its Legacies: An Introduction. *Politics & Society*, 45(2), 159–172.

De Jong. L. (2002). *The Collapse of a Colonial Society: The Dutch in Indonesia during the Second World War*. Leiden: KITLV Press.

Dell, M. and Olken, B. (2020). The Development Effects of the Extractive Colonial Economy: The Dutch Cultivation System in Java. *The Review of Economic Studies*, 87(1), 164–203.

Dhont, F., Marles, J., and Jukim, M. (2016). Memories of World War II: Oral History of Brunei Darussalam (December 1941 – June 1945). *Working Paper Series*, No. 25. Gadong, Brunei: Institute of Asian Studies, Universiti Brunei Darussalam.

Drea, E., Bradsher, G., Hanyok, R., et al. (2006). *Researching Japanese War Crimes Records: Introductory Essays*. Washington DC: Nazi War Crimes and Japanese Imperial Government Records Interagency Working Group.

Ducoroy, M. (1949). *Ma trahison en Indochine*. Paris: Les Éditions Internationales.

Dulay, D. (2022). The Search for Spices and Souls: Catholic Missions as Colonial State in the Philippines. *Comparative Political Studies*, 55(12), 2050–2085.

Duus, P. (1996). Imperialism without Colonies: The Vision of a Greater East Asia Co-prosperity Sphere. *Diplomacy and Statecraft*, 7(1), 54–72.

Duus, P., Myers, R., and Peattie, M. (eds.) (1996). *The Japanese Wartime Empire, 1931–1945*. Princeton, NJ: Princeton University Press.

Eaton, C. (2014). Communal Welfare Associations and the Agricultural Settlements of Wartime Singapore. Proceedings of the Fifth Conference of the Consortium for African and Asian Studies, Columbia University. (Accessed here, August 14, 2024 www.tufs.ac.jp/english/collaboration/caas/Proceedings_5th.html).

  (2018). *Governing Shōnan: The Japanese Administration of Wartime Singapore*. PhD Dissertation. New York, NY: Columbia University.

  (2023). Strategic Races: Understanding Racial Categories in Japanese-occupied Singapore. *Asian Ethnicity*, 24(2), 505–522.

Edington, C. (2016). Drug Detention and Human Rights in Post Doi Moi Vietnam. In Kim, D. and Singh, J. (eds.) *The Postcolonial World*. Abingdon: Routledge, pp. 325–242.

Edwards, P. (2006). The Tyranny of Proximity: Power and Mobility in Colonial Cambodia, 1863–1954. *Journal of Southeast Asian Studies*, 37(3), 421–443.

  (2007). *Cambodge: The Cultivation of a Nation, 1860–1945*. Honolulu, HI: University of Hawai'i Press.

Elsbree, W. (1953). *Japan's Role in Southeast Asian Nationalist Movements, 1940 to 1945*. Cambridge, MA: Harvard University Press.

References

Emmerson, D. (1984). "Southeast Asia": What's in a Name? *Journal of Southeast Asian Studies*, 15(1), 1–21.

Fanselow, F. (2014). The Anthropology of the State and the State of Anthropology in Brunei. *Journal of Southeast Asian Studies*, 45(1), 90–112.

Farrell, H. and Newman, A. (2019). Weaponized Interdependence: How Global Economic Networks Shape State Coercion. *International Security*, 44(1), 42–79.

Ferguson, J. (2015). Who's Counting? Ethnicity, Belonging, and the National Census in Burma/Myanmar. *Bijdragen Tot de Taal-, Land- En Volkenkunde*, 171(1), 1–28.

(2021). *Repossessing Shanland: Myanmar, Thailand, and a Nation-State Deferred*. Madison, WI: University of Wisconsin Press.

Fibiger, M. (2023). *Suharto's Cold War: Indonesia, Southeast Asia, and the World*. Oxford: Oxford University Press.

Fioretos, O., Falleti, T., and Sheingate, A. (2016). Historical Institutionalism in Political Science. In Fioretos, O., Falleti, T., and Sheingate, A. (eds.) *Oxford Handbook of Historical Institutionalism*. Oxford: Oxford University Press, pp. 3–28.

Firpo, C. (2016). *The Uprooted: Race, Children, and Imperialism in French Indochina, 1890–1980*. Honolulu, HI: University of Hawai'i Press.

Frei, H. (1996). Japan's Reluctant Decision to Occupy Portuguese Timor, 1 January 1942 – 20 February 1942. *Australian Historical Studies*, 27(107), 281–302

Freud, B. (2014). Organizing Autarky: Governor General Decoux's Development of a Substitution Economy in Indochina as a Means of Promoting Colonial Legitimacy. *SOJOURN: Journal of Social Issues in Southeast Asia*, 29(1), 96–131.

Friend, T. (1988). *The Blue-Eyed Friend: Japan against the West in Java and Luzon, 1942–1945*. Princeton, NJ: Princeton University Press.

Goodman, G. (1988). The Japanese Occupation of the Philippines: Commonwealth Sustained. *Philippine Studies*, 36(1), 98–104.

(ed.). (1991). *Japanese Cultural Policies in Southeast Asia during World War II*. London: MacMillan.

Go, J. (2024). Reverberations of Empire: How the Colonial Past Shapes the Present. *Social Science History*, 1–18.

Goscha, G. (2009). Widening the Colonial Encounter: Asian Connections Inside French Indochina during the Interwar Period. *Modern Asian Studies*, 43(5), 1189–1228.

Gotō, K. (2003). *Tensions of Empire: Japan and Southeast Asia in the Colonial and Postcolonial World*. Athens, OH: Ohio University Press.

References

Grandjean, P. (2004). *L'Indochine face au Japon 1940–1945: Decoux – de Gaulle, un malentendu fatal*. Paris: Editions L'Harmattan.

Gunn, G. (1988). *Political Struggles in Laos (1930–1954): Vietnamese Communist Power and the Lao Struggle for National Independence*. Bangkok: Editions Duang Kamol.

(2012). The Passing of Sihanouk: Monarchic Manipulation and the Search for Autonomy in the Kingdom of Cambodia. *Asia Pacific Journal, Japan Focus*, 10(1), 1–26.

(2014). *Rice Wars in Colonial Vietnam: The Great Famine and the Viet Minh Road to Power*. Lanham, MD: Rowman & Littlefield.

Guyot, D. (1966). *The Political Impact of the Japanese Occupation of Burma*. Ph.D. Dissertation. New Haven, CT: Yale University.

Han, L. P. (2009). The Beginning and Development of the Raffles Library in Singapore, 1823–1941: A Nineteenth-Century and Early Twentieth-Century British Colonial Enclave. *Library and Information History*, 25(4), 265–278.

Harper, T. (1999). *The End of Empire and the Making of Malaya*. Cambridge: Cambridge University Press.

(2007). A Long View on the Great Asian War. In Koh, D. (ed.) *Legacies of World War II in South and East Asia*. Singapore: Institute of Southeast Asian Studies, pp. 7–20.

Harrison, R. and Jackson, P. (2009). Introduction: Siam's/Thailand's Constructions of Modernity under the Influence of the Colonial West. *South East Asia Research*. 17(3), 325–360.

Hassan, M. (2021). *Regime Threats and State Solutions: Bureaucratic Loyalty and Embeddedness in Kenya*. Cambridge: Cambridge University Press.

Hedman, E. and Sidel, J. (2000). *Philippine Politics and Society in the Twentieth Century: Colonial Legacies, Post-Colonial Trajectories*. London: Routledge.

Helmke, G. and Levitsky, S. (2004). Informal Institutions and Comparative Politics: A Research Agenda. *Perspectives on Politics*, 2(4), 725–740.

Herzfeld, M. (2017). Thailand in a Larger Universe: The Lingering Consequences of Crypto-Colonialism. *Journal of Asian Studies*, 76(4), 887–906.

Hirofumi, H. (1998). Japanese Comfort Women in Southeast Asia. *Japan Forum*, 10(2), 211–219.

Hla Pe, U. (1961). *U Hla Pe's Narrative of the Japanese Occupation of Burma Recorded by U Khin*. Ithaca, NY: Cornell University Southeast Asia Program. Data Paper, No. 41.

Hodgkins, F. (2014). *From Syonan to Fuji-Go: The Story of the Catholic Settlement in Bahau in WWII Malaya*. Singapore: Select Publishing.

Howell, D. (2005). *Geographies of Identity in Nineteenth-Century Japan*. Berkeley, CA: University of California Press.

Hovinga, H. (2005). End of a Forgotten Drama: The Reception and Repatriation of Romusha after the Japanese Capitulation. In Kratsoka, P. (ed.) *Asian Labor in the Wartime Japanese Empire: Unknown Histories*. New York, NY: M.E. Sharpe, pp. 213–234.

Huang, Q. (2020). The Japanese Occupation of Singapore: Examining the Success of the Endau Settlement. *Emory Journal of Asian Studies*, 2, 1–20.

Huff, G. (2020a). *World War II and Southeast Asia: Economy and Society under Japanese Occupation*. Cambridge: Cambridge University Press.

(2020b). The Great Second World War Vietnam and Java Famines. *Modern Asian Studies*, 54(2), 618–653.

Huff, G. and Majima, S. (eds.). (2011). The Japanese Occupation of South East Asia during the Second World War. *South East Asia Research*, 19(4), 855–877.

(2018). *World War II Singapore: The Chosabu Reports on Syonan*. Singapore: National University of Singapore Press.

Hussainmiya, B. (2003). Resuscitating Nationalism: Brunei under Japanese Military Administration, 1941–1945. In Shimizu, A. and Bremen, J. (eds.) *Wartime Japanese Anthropology in Asia and the Pacific*. Senri Ethnological Studies, 65. Osaka: National Museum of Ethnology, pp. 273–297.

Hussin, I. (2016). *The Politics of Islamic Law: Local Elites, Colonial Authority and the Making of the Muslim State*. Chicago, IL: University of Chicago Press.

Hutchcroft, P. (1988). *Booty Capitalism: The Politics of Banking in the Philippines*. Ithaca, NY: Cornell University Press.

Ikehata, S. and Jose, R. (1999). (eds.). *The Philippines under Japan: Occupation Policy and Reaction*. Quezon City: Ateneo de Manila University Press.

Ikeya, C. (2011). *Refiguring Women, Colonialism, and Modernity in Burma*. Honolulu, HI: University of Hawai'i Press.

Ileto, R. (2004). The "Unfinished Revolution" of 1943? Rethinking Japanese Occupation and the Postwar Nation-Building in the Philippines. *Sophia AGLOS Working Paper Series*, 1, 1–22.

(2007). World War II: Transient and Enduring Legacies for the Philippines. In Koh, D. (ed.) *Legacies of World War II in South and East Asia*. Singapore: Institute of Southeast Asian Studies, pp. 74–91.

Iriye, A. (1993). *The Cambridge History of American Foreign Relations, Vol. III The Globalizing of America, 1913–1945*. New York, NY: Cambridge University Press.

Ivarsson, S. (1999). Towards a New Laos: Lao Nhay and the Campaign for National "Reawakening" in Laos, 1941–45. In Evans, G. (ed.) *Laos: Culture and Society*, Chiang Mai: Silkworm Books, pp. 61–78.

Iwamoto, H. (1999). *Nanshin: Japanese Settlers in Papua and New Guinea, 1890–1949*. Canberra: Australian National University. The Journal of Pacific History.

Jaffrey, S. (2019). *Leveraging the Leviathan: Politics of Impunity and the Rise of Vigilantism in Democratic Indonesia*. Ph.D. Dissertation. Chicago, IL: University of Chicago.

Jennings, E. (2011). *Imperial Heights: Dalat and the Making and Undoing of French Indochina*. Berkeley, CA: University of California Press.

Kahin, G. (1952). *Nationalism and Revolution in Indonesia*. Ithaca, NY: Cornell University Press.

Kammen, D. (2015). *Three Centuries of Conflict in East Timor*. New Brunswick, NJ: Rutgers University Press.

Kawashima, M. (1996). The Records of the Former Japanese Army Concerning the Japanese Occupation of the Philippines. *Journal of Southeast Asian Studies*, 27(1), 124–131.

Keith, C. (2012). *Catholic Vietnam: A Church from Empire to Nation*. Berkeley, CA: University of California Press.

(2017). Vietnamese Collaboration in Vichy France. *Journal of Asian Studies*, 76(4), 987–1008.

Kerkvliet, B. (2002). *The Huk Rebellion: A Study of Peasant Revolt in the Philippines*. Lanham, MD: Rowman and Littlefield.

Keyes, C. (1994). Communist Revolution and the Buddhist Past in Cambodia. In Keyes, C., Kendall, L., & Hardacre, H. (eds.) *Asian Visions of Authority: Religion and the Modern States of East and Southeast Asia*. Honolulu, HI: University of Hawai'i Press, 43–73.

Kim, D. (2020). *Empires of Vice: The Rise of Opium Prohibition across Southeast Asia*. Princeton, NJ: Princeton University Press.

Kingsberg, M. (2013). *Moral Nation: Modern Japan and Narcotics in Global History*. Berkeley: University of California Press.

Kintanar, T., Aquino, C., Camagay, L. and Arinto, P. (2006). *Kuwentong Bayan: Noong Panahon ng Hapon: Everyday Life in a Time of War*. Quezon City: The University of Philippines Press.

Koh, D. (ed.). (2007). *Legacies of World War II in South and East Asia*. Singapore: Institute of Southeast Asian Studies.

Kohli, A. (2020). *Imperialism and the Developing World: How Britain and the United States Shaped the Global Periphery*. New York, NY: Oxford University Press.

Kratoska, P. (ed.). (1998). *Food Supplies and the Japanese Occupation in South-East Asia*. New York, NY: St. Martins's Press.

(ed.). (2002). *Southeast Asian Minorities in the Wartime Japanese Empire*. Abingdon: RoutledgeCurzon.

(ed.). (2005). *Asian Labor in the Wartime Japanese Empire: Unknown Histories*. New York, NY: M.E. Sharpe.

(2018). *The Japanese Occupation of Malaya and Singapore, 1941–45: A Social and Economic History*. 2nd ed. Singapore: National University of Singapore Press.

Kuhonta, E. (2014). Southeast Asia and Comparative-Historical Analysis: Region, Theory and Ontology on a Wide Canvas. *Pacific Affairs*, 87(3), 485–507.

Kuhonta, E. and Truong, N. (2020). The Institutional Roots of Defective Democracy in the Philippines. In Croissant, A. and Hellmann, O. (eds.) *Stateness and Democracy in East Asia*, Cambridge: Cambridge University Press, pp. 153–178.

Kuipers, N. (2022). The Long-Run Consequences of the Opium Concessions for Out-Group Animosity on Java. *World Politics*, 74(3): 405–442.

Kurasawa, A. (1988). *Mobilization and Control: A Study of Social Change in Rural Java, 1942–1945*. Ph.D Dissertation. Ithaca, NY: Cornell University.

Kusumaryati, V. (2021). Freeport and the States: Politics of Corporations and Contemporary Colonialism in West Papua. *Comparative Studies in Society and History*, 63(4): 881–910.

Kwartanada, D. (2002). Competition, Patriotism and Collaboration: The Chinese Businessmen of Yogyakarta between the 1930s and 1945. *Journal of Southeast Asian Studies*, 33(2), 257–277.

Laffan, M. (2021). The Forgotten Jihad under Japan: Muslim Reformism and the Promise of Indonesian Independence. *Journal of the Economic and Social History of the Orient*, 64(1–2), 125–161.

Laitin, D. and Ramachandran, R. (in press). The Historical Sources of Language Policy. *Journal of Politics*. https://doi.org/10.1086/732951.

Lanzona, V. (2009). *Amazons of the Huk Rebellion: Gender, Sex, and Revolution in the Philippines*. Madison, WI: The University of Wisconsin Press.

Lebra, J. (ed.). (1975). *Japan's Greater East Asia Co-Prosperity Sphere in World War II: Selected Readings and Documents*. Oxford: Oxford University Press.

Lebra, J. (1977). *Japanese-Trained Armies in Southeast Asia: Independence and Volunteer Forces in World War II*. New York, NY: Columbia University Press.

Lee, G. (2016). Collecting the Scattered Remains: The Raffles Library and Museum. *BiblioAsia*, 12(1), 39–45.

Lentz, C. (2019). *Contested Territory: Dien Bien Phu and the Making of Northwest Vietnam*. New Haven, CT: Yale University Press.

Leow, R. (2016). *Taming Babel: Language and the Making of Malaysia*. Cambridge: Cambridge University Press.

Lewis, S. L. (2012). Rotary International's 'Acid Test': Multi-ethnic Associational Life in 1930s Southeast Asia. *Journal of Global History*, 7(2), 302–324.

Li, T. (2017). The Price of Un/Freedom: Indonesia's Colonial and Contemporary Plantation Labor Regimes. *Comparative Studies in Society and History*, 59(2), 245–276.

Lim, P. and Wong, D. (2000). *War and Memory in Malaysia and Singapore*. Singapore: Institute of Southeast Asian Studies

Linkhoeva, T. (2020). *Revolution Goes East: Imperial Japan and Soviet Communism*. Ithaca, NY: Cornell University Press.

Lipsky, M. (1980). *Street-Level Bureaucracy: The Dilemmas of the Individual in Public Service*. New York, NY: Russell Sage Foundation.

Liu, A. (2015). *Standardizing Diversity: The Political Economy of Language Regimes*. Philadelphia, PA: University of Pennsylvania Press.

Liu, A. and Selway, J. (2021). Explaining Identity Formation in Asia. *Asian Politics and Policy*, 13(1), 6–17.

Loh, K. S., Koh, E., and Dobbs, S. (eds.). (2013). *Oral History in Southeast Asia: Memories and Fragments*. New York, NY: Palgrave MacMillan.

Loos, T. (2008). A History of Sex and the State in Southeast Asia: Class, Intimacy, and Invisibility. *Citizenship Studies*, 12(1), 27–43.

  (2018). "Competitive Colonialisms: Siam and the Malay Muslim South," in *The Ambiguous Allure of the West: Traces of the Colonial in Thailand*, 75–91, (eds.) D. Chakrabarty, R. Harrison and P. Jackson. Ithaca, NY: Cornell University Press.

Luyt, B. (2009). Colonialism, Ethnicity, and Geopolitics in the Development of the Singapore National Library. *Libraries & the Cultural Record*, 44(4), 418–433.

Mabberley, D. (2000). A Tropical Botanist Finally Vindicated. *Gardens' Bulletin Singapore*, 52, 1–4.

Maekawa, K. (2002). The Pontianak Incidents and the Ethnic Chinese in Wartime Western Borneo. In Kratoska, P. (ed.) *Southeast Asian Minorities in the Wartime Japanese Empire*. Abingdon: RoutledgeCurzon, pp. 153–169.

Mahoney, J. and Thelen, K. (2010). *Explaining Institutional Change: Ambiguity, Agency, and Power*. New York, NY: Cambridge University Press.

Maier, C. (2023). *The Project-State and its Rivals: A New History of the Twentieth and Twenty-First Centuries*. Cambridge, MA: Harvard University Press.

Manela, E. (2007). *The Wilsonian Moment: Self-Determination and the International Origins of Anticolonial Nationalism*. Princeton, NJ: Princeton University Press.

Manickam, S. (2014). Bridging the Race Barrier: Between "Sakai" and "Malay" in the Census Categorizations of British Malaya. *Asian Studies Review*, 38(3): 367–384.

Masucol, E., Jap, J., and Liu, A. (2022). Islands Apart: Explaining the Chinese Experience in the Philippines. *Comparative Government*, (4): 1–16.

Matthiessen, S. (2016). *Japanese Pan-Asianism and the Philippines from the Late Nineteenth Century to the End of World War II: Going to the Philippines Is Like Coming Home?* Leiden: Brill.

Mark, E. (2014). The Perils of Co-Prosperity: Takeda Rintarō, Occupied Southeast Asia, and the Seductions of Postcolonial Empire. *American Historical Review*, 119(4), 1184–1206.

(2018). *Japan's Occupation of Java in the Second World War: A Transnational History*. London: Bloomsbury Academic.

Marr, D. (1980). World War II and the Vietnamese Revolution. In McCoy, A. (ed.) *Southeast Asia under Japanese Occupation*. New Haven, CT: Yale University Southeast Asia Studies, pp. 125–158.

(1995). *Vietnam 1945: The Quest for Power*. Berkeley, CA: University of California Press.

(2013). *Vietnam: State, War, and Revolution, 1945–1946*. Berkeley, CA: University of California Press.

Maung, M. (1989). *Burmese Nationalist Movements, 1940–1948*. Edinburgh: Kiscadale Press.

Maw, B. (1968). *Breakthrough in Burma: Memoirs of a Revolution, 1939–1946*. New Haven, CT: Yale University Press.

McCoy, A. (ed.). (1980a). *Southeast Asia under Japanese Occupation*. New Haven, CT: Yale University Southeast Asia Studies.

(ed.). (1980b). 'Politics by Other Means': World War II in the Western Visayas, Philippines. In McCoy, A. (ed.) *Southeast Asia under Japanese Occupation*. New Haven, CT: Yale University Southeast Asia Studies, pp. 191–245.

(2009). *Policing America's Empire: The United States, the Philippines, and the Rise of the Surveillance State*. Madison, WI: The University of Wisconsin Press.

Melber, T. (2016). The Labour Recruitment of Local Inhabitants as Rōmusha in Japanese- Occupied South East Asia. *International Review of Social History*, 61(S24), 165–185.

Menchik, J. (2014). Productive Intolerance: Godly Nationalism in Indonesia. *Comparative Studies in Society and History*, 56(3), 591–621

Mendoza, M. (2021). When Institutions Reinforce Regional Divides: Comparing Christian and Muslim Colonial Education Policies in the Philippines. *Asian Politics & Policy*, 13(1), 90–104.

Mimura, J. (2011a). *Planning for Empire: Reform Bureaucrats and the Japanese Wartime State*. Ithaca, NY: Cornell University Press.

(2011b). Japan's New Order and Greater East Asia Co-Prosperity Sphere: Planning for Empire. *Asia Pacific Journal, Japan Focus*, 9(3), 1–12.

Minohara, T. and Dawley, E. (eds.) (2020). *Beyond Versailles: The 1919 Moment and a New Order in East Asia*. Lanham, MD: Lexington Book

Mitsuomi, I. and Fernando, J. (2014). Early Uses and Conceptualization of the Term "Southeast Asia." *SEJARAH: Jurnal Jabatan Sejarah Universiti Malaya*, 23(2), 157–174.

Mitter, R. (2000). *The Manchurian Myth: Nationalism, Resistance, and Collaboration in Modern China*. Berkeley, CA: University of California Press.

Monnais, L. (2019). *The Colonial Life of Pharmaceuticals: Medicines and Modernity in Vietnam*. Cambridge: Cambridge University Press.

Morgan, K. and Orloff, A. (2017). *The Many Hands of the State: Theorizing Political Authority and Social Control*. New York, NY: Cambridge University Press

Morris-Suzuki, T. (1998). Debating Racial Science in Wartime Japan. *Osiris*, 13(1), 354–375.

Morris-Suzuki, T. (2015). You Don't Want to Know About the Girls? The "Comfort Women," the Japanese Military and Allied Forces in the Asia-Pacific War. *Asia-Pacific Journal*, 13(2), 1–11.

Mukoyama, N. (2020). Colonial Origins of the Resource Curse : Endogenous Sovereignty and Authoritarianism in Brunei. *Democratization*, 27(2), 224–242.

Mus, P. (1946). l'Indochine en 1945. *Politique étrangère*, 5(11), 433–464.

Nakahara, M. (2001). "Comfort Women" in Malaysia. *Critical Asian Studies*, 33(4), 581–589.

Nakahara, M. (2015). Malayan Labor on the Thailand-Burma Railway. In Kratsoka, P. (ed.) *Asian Labor in the Wartime Japanese Empire: Unknown Histories*. New York: M.E. Sharpe, pp. 249–264.

Nakamura, M. (1970). General Imamura and the Early Period of Japanese Occupation. *Indonesia*, 10, 1–26.

Nakamura, T. (1996). The Yen Bloc, 1931–1941. In Duus, P., Myers, R. and Peattie, M. (ed.) *The Japanese Wartime Empire, 1931–1945*. Princeton, NJ: Princeton University Press, pp. 171–186.

Nam, S. (2020). Fiction, Fraud, and Formality: The Legal Infrastructure of Property Speculation in Cambodia. *Critical Asian Studies*, 52(3), 364–377.

Namba, C. (2012). *Français et Japonais en Indochine (1940–1945): Colonisation, Propagande ET Rivalité Culturelle*. Paris: Karthala.

(2015). An Introduction to French Research and Historical Sources Concerning Indochina under French-Japanese Rule. In Shiraishi, M. (ed.) *Indochina, Thailand, Japan and France during World War II: Overview of Existing*

Literature and Related Documents for the Future Development of Research. Tokyo: Waseda University Institute of Asia-Pacific Studies, pp. 255–264.

Naseemullah, A. (2022). *Patchwork States: The Historical Roots of Subnational Conflict and Competition in South Asia*. Cambridge: Cambridge University Press.

Naw, A. (2001). *Aung San and the Struggle for Burmese Independence*. Chiang Mai: Silkworm Books.

Nguyen, P. V. (2017). The Vietnamization of Personalism: The Role of Missionaries in the Spread of Personalism in Vietnam, 1930–1961. *French Colonial History*, 17, 103–134.

Nitz, K. (1983). Japanese Military Policy Towards French Indochina during the Second World War: The Road to the "Meigo Sakusen" (9 March 1945). *Journal of Southeast Asian Studies*, 14(2), 328–353.

(1984). Independence without Nationalists? The Japanese and Vietnamese Nationalism during the Japanese Period. *Journal of Southeast Asian Studies*, 15(1), 108–133.

Ooi, K. G. (ed.). (1998). *Japanese Empire in the Tropics: Selected Documents and Reports of the Japanese Period in Sarawak, Northwest Borneo, 1941–1945*. Athens, OH: Ohio University Center for International Studies.

Ooi, K. G. (1999). *Rising Sun over Borneo: The Japanese Occupation of Sarawak, 1941–1945*. New York, NJ: St. Martin's Press.

(2006). The "Slapping Monster" and Other Stories: Recollections of the Japanese Occupation (1941–1945) of Borneo through Autobiographies, Biographies, Memoirs, and Other Ego-Documents. *Journal of Colonialism and Colonial History*, 7(3).

(2011). *The Japanese Occupation of Borneo, 1941–1945*. London and New York: Routledge.

(2013). *Post-War Borneo, 1945–1950: Nationalism, Empire, and State-Building*. London: Routledge.

Ōta, T. (1967). *Biruma ni okeru Nihon Gunsei-shi no Kenkyu* [*Research in the History of the Japanese Military Administration of Burma*]. Tokyo: Yoshikawa Kobunkan.

Paine, S. (2012). *The Wars for Asia, 1911–1949*. New York, NY: Cambridge University Press.

Peattie, M. (1984). Japanese Attitudes Toward Colonialism, 1895–1945. In Myers, R. and Peattie, M. (eds.) *The Japanese Colonial Empire, 1895–1945*. Princeton, NJ: Princeton University Press, pp. 80–127.

(1992). *Nan'yō: The Rise and Fall of the Japanese in Micronesia, 1885–1945*. Honolulu, HI: University of Hawai'i Press.

(1996). Nanshin: The "Southward Advance," 1931–1941, as a Prelude to the Japanese Occupation of Southeast Asia. In Duus, P., Myers, R. and Peattie, M. (eds.). *The Japanese Wartime Empire, 1931–1945*. Princeton, NJ: Princeton University Press, pp. 189–242.

Pedersen, S. (2015). *The Guardians: The League of Nations and the Crisis of Empire*. Oxford: Oxford University Press.

Pelletier, A. (2019). *Radical Leaders: Status, Competition, and Violent Islamic Mobilization in Indonesia*. PhD Thesis, Toronto: University of Toronto.

Pepinsky, T. (2016). Colonial Migration and the Origins of Governance: Theory and Evidence From Java. *Comparative Political Studies*, 49(9), 1201–1237.

Quimpo, N. (2005). Review: Oligarchic Patrimonialism, Bossism, Electoral Clientelism, and Contested Democracy in the Philippines. *Comparative Politics*, 37(2), 229–250.

Rafael, V. (1991). Anticipating Nationhood: Collaboration and Rumor in the Japanese Occupation of Manila. *Diaspora*, 1(1), 67–82.

(2016). *Motherless Tongues: The Insurgency of Language Amid Wars of Translation*. Durham, NC: Duke University Press.

Raffin, A. (2002). Easternization Meets Westernization: Patriotic Youth Organizations in French Indochina during World War II, *French Politics, Culture, and Society*, 20(2), 121–140.

(2005). *Youth Mobilization in Vichy Indochina and Its Legacies, 1940 to 1970*. Lanham, MD: Lexington Books.

(2012). Youth Mobilization and Ideology: Cambodia from the Late Colonial Era to the Pol Pot Regime. *Critical Asian Studies*, 44(3), 391–418.

Ramnath, K. (2023). *Boats in a Storm: Law, Migration, and Decolonization in South and Southeast Asia, 1942–1962*. Palo Alto, CA: Stanford University Press.

Recto, C. (1946). *Three Years of Enemy Occupation: The Issue of Political Collaboration in the Philippines*. Manila: People's Publishers.

Reid, A. (1981). The Birth of the Republic in Sumatra. *Indonesia*, 12, 21–46.

(1975). The Japanese Occupation and Rival Indonesian Elites: Northern Sumatra in 1942. *Journal of Asian Studies*, 35(1), 49–61.

Reid, A. and Akira, O. (1986). *The Japanese Experience in Indonesia: Selected Memoirs of 1942–1945*. Athens, OH: Ohio University Press.

Reith, G. M. (1892). *Handbook to Singapore: With Map and a Plan of the Botanic Gardens*. Singapore: Singapore and Straits Printing Office.

Ren, C. (2023). Global Circulation of Low-end Expertise: Knowledge, Hierarchy, and Labor Migration in a Burmese Oilfield. *History of Science*, 61(4), 561–587.

Reyes, A. (2021). Postcolonial Semiotics. *Annual Review of Anthropology*, 50, 291–307.

Reynolds, B. (1994). *Thailand and Japan's Southern Advance, 1940–1945*. New York, NY: St. Martin's Press.

(1996). Anomaly or Model? Independent Thailand's Role in Japan's Asian Strategy, 1941–1943. In *The Japanese Wartime Empire, 1931–1945*. Edited by Duus, P., Myers, R. and Peattie, M. Princeton, NJ: Princeton University Press, pp. 243–273.

(2004). Phibun Songkhram and Thai Nationalism in the Fascist Era. *European Journal of East Asian Studies*, 3(1), 99–134.

Ricks, J. and Liu, A. (2018). Process-Tracing Research Designs: A Practical Guide. *PS: Political Science & Politics*, 51(4), 842–846.

Rithmire, M. (2023). *Precarious Ties : Business and the State in Authoritarian Asia*. Oxford: Oxford University Press.

Rochet, C. (1946). *Pays Lao: Le Laos dans la tourmente*. Paris: Jean Vigneau.

Rōyama, M. and Takéuchi, T. (1967). The Philippine Polity: A Japanese View. Translated by T. Takéuchi; Edited by Friend, T. New Haven, CT: Yale University, Southeast Asia Studies Monograph Series, 12.

Saada, E. (2012). *Empire's Children: Race, Filiation, and Citizenship in the French Colonies*. Chicago, IL: University of Chicago Press.

Sadan, M. (2013). Ethnic Armies and Ethnic Conflict in Burma: Reconsidering the History of Colonial Militarization in the Kachin Region of Burma during the Second World War. *South East Asia Research*. 21(4), 601–626.

Saito, M. (2017). On Wartime Money Finance in the Japanese Occupied Territories during the Pacific War: The Case of Instant Reserve Banks and Bad Central Banks. Discussion Paper, 3. Hitotsubashi University: 1–27. Accessed here on August 17, 2024. https://ideas.repec.org/p/hit/econdp/2017-03.html.

Sand, J. (2014). Subaltern Imperialists: The New Historiography of the Japanese Empire. *Past and Present*, 225, 273–288.

Sani, H. (2019). *Elite Politics, Jurisdictional Conflicts and the Legacy of Colonial State Building in Malaysia*. PhD dissertation. Chicago, IL: University of Chicago.

Sareen, T. R. (2004). Subhas Chandra Bose, Japan and British Imperialism. *European Journal of East Asian Studies*, 3(1), 69–97.

Sasges, G. and Cheshier, S. (2012). Competing Legacies: Rupture and Continuity in Vietnamese Political Economy. *South East Asia Research*, 20(1), 5–33.

Sato, S. (1994). *War, Nationalism, and Peasants: Java under the Japanese Occupation, 1942–45*. New York, NY: M.E. Sharpe.

Satoshi, N. (2018). *Japan's Colonial Moment in Southeast Asia 1942–1945*. London: Routledge.

Seet, K. K. (1983). *A Place for the People: The Story of a National Library.* Singapore: Times Books International.

Shinozaki, M. (1975). *Syonan-My Story: The Japanese Occupation of Singapore.* Canberra: Asia-Pacific Press.

Shiraishi, M. (ed.). (2015). *Indochina, Thailand, Japan and France during World War II: Overview of the Existing Literature and Related Documents for the Future Development of Research.* Tokyo: Waseda University Institute for Asia-Pacific Studies.

Shiraishi, S. and Shiraishi, T. (eds.). (1993). *The Japanese in Colonial Southeast Asia.* Ithaca, NY: Cornell University Press.

Shirane, S. (2022). *Imperial Gateway: Colonial Taiwan and Japan's Expansion into South China and Southeast Asia.* Ithaca, NY: Cornell University Press.

Shoji, I. (2015). Historical Documents Relating to the Japanese Occupation of Malaya. *Journal of Malaysian Branch of the Royal Asiatic Society*, 88 (308), 87–117.

Sidel, J. (1999). *Capital, Coercion, and Crime: Bossism in the Philippines.* Palo Alto CA: Stanford University Press.

Sidel, J. (2008). Social Origins of Dictatorship and Democracy Revisited: Colonial State and Chinese Immigrant in the Making of Modern Southeast Asia. *Comparative Politics*, 40(2), 127–147.

  (2021). *Republicanism, Communism, Islam: Cosmopolitan Origins of Revolution in Southeast Asia.* Ithaca, NY: Cornell University Press.

Silverstein, J. (1958). Politics in the Shan State: The Question of Succession from the Union of Burma. *Journal of Asian Studies*, 18(1), 43–57.

Simmons, E. and Smith, N. (eds.). (2021). *Rethinking Comparison: Innovative Methods for Qualitative Political Inquiry.* Cambridge: Cambridge University Press.

Simpser, A., Slater, D. and Wittenberg, J. (2018). Dead But Not Gone: Contemporary Legacies of Communism, Imperialism, and Authoritarianism. *Annual Review of Political Science*, 21, 419–439.

Slater, D. (2010). *Ordering Power: Contentious Politics and Authoritarian Leviathans in Southeast Asia.* New York, NY: Cambridge University Press.

Slater, D., Way, L., Lachapelle, J. and Casey, A. (2023). The Origins of Military Supremacy in Dictatorships. *Journal of Democracy*, 34(3), 5–20.

Sluimers, L. (1996). The Japanese Military and Indonesian Independence. *Journal of Southeast Asian Studies*, 27(1), 19–36.

Smith, R. (1978). The Japanese Period in Indochina and the Coup of 9 March 1945. *Journal of Southeast Asian Studies*, 9(2), 268–301.

Soifer. H. (2012). The Casual Logic of Critical Junctures. *Comparative Political Studies*, 45(12), 1572–1597.

Steinberg, D. (1965). Jose P. Laurel: A "Collaborator" Misunderstood. *Journal of Asian Studies*, 24(4), 651–665.

(1967). *Philippine Collaboration in World War II*. Ann Arbor, MI: University of Michigan Press.

Stoler, A. (1985). *Capitalism and Confrontation in Sumatra's Plantation Belt, 1870–1979*. New Haven, CT: Yale University Press.

(2008). Imperial Debris: Reflections on Ruins and Ruination. *Cultural Anthropology*, 23(2), 191–219.

Strate, S. (2015). *The Lost Territories: Thailand's History of National Humiliation*. Honolulu, HI: University of Hawai'i Press.

Sugarman, M. (2018). Reclaiming Rangoon: (Post-)Imperial Urbanism and Poverty, 1920–62. *Modern Asian Studies*, 52(6), 1856–1887.

Suryanarayan, P. (2024). Endogenous State Capacity. *Annual Review of Political Science*, 27, 223–243.

Tagliacozzo, E. (2005). *Secret Trades, Porous Borders: Smuggling and States Along a Southeast Asian Frontier, 1865–1915*. New Haven, CT: Yale University Press.

Tajima, Y. (2014). *The Institutional Origins of Communal Violence: Indonesia's Transition from Authoritarian Rule*. Cambridge: Cambridge University Press.

Takagi, Y. (2016). *Central Banking as State Building: Policymakers and Their Nationalism in the Philippines, 1933–1964*. Chicago, IL: University of Chicago Press.

Tarling, N. (2001). *A Sudden Rampage: The Japanese Occupation of Southeast Asia, 1941–1945*. Honolulu, HI: University of Hawai'i Press.

Taylor, R. (1980). Burma in the Anti-Fascist War. In McCoy, A. (ed.) *Southeast Asia Under Japanese Occupation*. New Haven, CT: Yale University Southeast Asia Studies, pp. 159–190.

(2009). *The State in Myanmar*. Singapore: University of Hawai'i Press.

Taylor, R. (2009). *The State in Myanmar*. Honolulu: University of Hawai'i Press.

Terami-Wada, M. (1990). The Japanese Propaganda Corp in the Philippines. *Philippine Studies*, 38(3), 279–300.

(2014). *Sakdalista's Struggle for Philippine Independence, 1930–1945*. Quezon City: Ateneo de Manila University Press.

Thomas, M. and Thompson, A. (2014). Empire and Globalisation: From "High" Imperialism to Decolonization. *International History Review*, 36(1), 142–170.

Trager, F. (ed.). (1971). *Burma: Japanese Military Administration, Selected Documents, 1941–1945*. Translated from Japanese by W. Z. Yoon. Philadelphia, PA: University of Pennsylvania Press.

Tran, M. V. (1996). Japan and Vietnam's Caodaists: A Wartime Relationship (1939–1945). *Journal of Southeast Asian Studies*, 27(1), 179–193.

Tremml-Werner, B. (2015). *Spain, China, and Japan in Manila, 1571–1644: Local Comparisons and Global Connections*. Amsterdam: Amsterdam University Press.

Tsuchiya, K. (2019a). Representing Timor: Histories, Geo-bodies, and Belonging, 1860s–2018. *Journal of Southeast Asian Studies*, 50(3), 365–386.

(2019b). Indigenization of the Pacific War in Timor Island: A Multi-Language Study of its Contexts and Impact. *War and Society*, 38(1), 19–40.

Tsuda, K. (2020). Kung Yung Pao: The Only Daily Newspaper for the Ethnic Chinese in Java during Japanese Occupation. Taipei: Transmission Books and Microinfo.

Turnbull, M. (1989). *A History of Singapore, 1819–1988*, 2nd ed. Singapore: Oxford University Press.

Turnell, S. (2011). Myanmar's Fifty-Year Authoritarian Trap. *Journal of International Affairs*, 65(1), 79–92.

Turnell, S. and Bradford, W. (2009). Paper Money in Burma: Creation, War, and Restoration. Working Paper, "Paper Money in Theory and Practice in History" Conference, Barnard College, Columbia University.

Uchida, J. (2016). From Island Nation to Oceanic Empire: A Vision of Japanese Expansion from the Periphery. *Journal of Japanese Studies*, 42(1), 57–90.

Gardens Bulletin of Singapore. (1946). The Singapore Botanic Garden During 1941–1946. *The Gardens' Bulletin, Singapore*, 11(4), 263–265.

Vltchek, A. and Idira, R. (2006). *Exile: Pramoedya Ananta Toer in conversation with Andre Vltcheck and Rossie Indira*. Chicago, IL: Haymarket Books.

Vu, T. (2010). *Paths to Development in Asia: South Korea, Vietnam, China, and Indonesia*. Cambridge: Cambridge University Press.

(2014). Triumphs or Tragedies: A New Perspective on the Vietnamese Revolution. *Journal of Southeast Asian Studies*, 45(2), 236–257.

Walker, K. (2012). Intimate Interactions: Eurasian Family Histories in Colonial Penang. *Modern Asian Studies*, 46(2), 303–329.

Weiss, M. (2020). *Roots of Resilience: Party Machines and Grassroots Politics in Southeast Asia*. Ithaca, NY: Cornell University Press.

Werner, Y. (1981). *Peasant Politics and Religious Sectarianism: Peasant and Priest in the Cao Dai in Viet Nam*. New Haven: Yale University, Southeast Asia Studies, Monograph Series, 23.

White, N., Barwise, J., and Yacob, S. (2020). Economic Opportunity and Strategic Dolemma in Colonial Development: Britain, Japan and Malaya's Iron Ore, 1920s to 1950s. *International History Review*, 42(2), 424–446.

Winichakul, T. (1994). *Siam Mapped: A History of the Geobody of a Nation*. Honolulu, HI: University of Hawai'i Press.

Yano, T. (1975). *Nanshin no Keifu [The Genealogy of the Southern Advance]*. Tokyo: Chūōkōron-sha.

Yellen, J. (2019). *The Greater East Asia Co-Prosperity Sphere: When Total Empire Met Total War*. Ithaca, NY: Cornell University Press.

Yoon, W. Z. (1978). Military Expediency: A Determining Factor in the Japanese Policy regarding Burmese Independence. *Journal of Southeast Asian Studies*, 9(2), 248–267.

Yoshizawa, M. (1992). The Nishihara Mission in Hanoi, July 1940. In Shiraishi, T. and Furuta, M. (eds.) *Indochina in the 1940s and 1950s*. Ithaca, NY: Cornell University Press, pp. 9–54.

Young, L. (1998).*Japan's Total Empire: Manchuria and the Culture of Wartime Imperialism*. Berkeley, CA: University of California Press.

  (2017). When Fascism Met Empire in Japanese-occupied Manchuria. *Journal of Global History*, 12, 274–296.

Yu-Jose, L. (1996). World War II and the Japanese in the Prewar Philippines. *Journal of Southeast Asian Studies*, 27(1), 64–81.

Zaide, G. and Zaide, S. (1990). *Documentary Sources of Philippine History*, vol. 1. Manila: National Book Store.

Zhao, J. (2003). The Looting of Books in Nanjing. In Translated from Chinese by P. Li. In Li, P. (ed.) *Japanese War Crimes: The Search for Justice*. New Brunswick, NJ: Transaction Publishers, pp. 281–287.

Acknowledgments

I am grateful to the Asian Studies Program at Georgetown University's School of Foreign Service, for our intellectual community and the opportunity to teach a class, Colonial Legacies in Southeast Asia, which partly inspired this Element. I owe especial thanks to my brilliant, thoughtful, and relentlessly curious students from this class: Hythem Al-Mulla, Fan (Pauline) Bu, Akaisha Cook, Jane Cox, Heidi Kang, Andreyka Natalegawa, Ayano (Alexis) Terai, and Sophie Wright. My research was generously supported by a Silvers Grant from the Robert B. Silvers Foundation, and drafts of this Element have benefited from the engagement of audiences at the Joint Center for History and Economics Seminar at Harvard University, the Political Violence Workshop at Yale University, the Friday Forum at the Center for Southeast Asian Studies at the University of Wisconsin-Madison, and the Gatty Lecture Series at the Southeast Asia Program at Cornell University. I am also deeply grateful to Sunil Amrith, Nick Cheesman, Ema Eguchi, Franziska Exeler, Chris Han, Tim Harper, Matthew Koo, Veronika Kusumaryati, Jean Lachapelle, Jessica Li, Amy Liu, Dann Naseemullah, Tyrell Haberkorn, Miriam Kingsberg, Paul Kratoska, Tom Pepinsky, Emma Rothschild, Bushra Shaikh, Dan Slater, Tiffany Tam, Kirsty Walker, Thongchai Winichakul, and Minh Vu for invaluable help at various stages of this Element's development, as well as to the series editors Ed Aspinall and Meredith Weiss and anonymous reviewers. All errors and shortcomings remain solely my own.

Cambridge Elements

Politics and Society in Southeast Asia

Edward Aspinall
Australian National University

Edward Aspinall is a professor of politics at the Coral Bell School of Asia-Pacific Affairs, Australian National University. A specialist of Southeast Asia, especially Indonesia, much of his research has focused on democratisation, ethnic politics and civil society in Indonesia and, most recently, clientelism across Southeast Asia.

Meredith L. Weiss
University at Albany, SUNY

Meredith L. Weiss is Professor of Political Science at the University at Albany, SUNY. Her research addresses political mobilization and contention, the politics of identity and development, and electoral politics in Southeast Asia, with particular focus on Malaysia and Singapore.

About the Series

The Elements series Politics and Society in Southeast Asia includes both country-specific and thematic studies on one of the world's most dynamic regions. Each title, written by a leading scholar of that country or theme, combines a succinct, comprehensive, up-to-date overview of debates in the scholarly literature with original analysis and a clear argument.

Cambridge Elements

Politics and Society in Southeast Asia

Elements in the Series

Civil Society in Southeast Asia: Power Struggles and Political Regimes
Garry Rodan

The Meaning of Democracy in Southeast Asia: Liberalism, Egalitarianism and Participation
Diego Fossati and Ferran Martinez i Coma

Organized Labor in Southeast Asia
Teri L. Caraway

The Philippines: From 'People Power' to Democratic Backsliding
Mark R. Thompson

Contesting Social Welfare in Southeast Asia
Andrew Rosser and John Murphy

The Politics of Cross-Border Mobility in Southeast Asia
Michele Ford

Myanmar: A Political Lexicon
Nick Cheesman

Courts and Politics in Southeast Asia
Björn Dressel

Thailand: Contestation, Polarization, and Democratic Regression
Prajak Kongkirati

Social Media and Politics in Southeast Asia
Merlyna Lim

State and Sub-state Nationalism in Southeast Asia
Jacques Bertrand

Rethinking Colonial Legacies Across Southeast Asia: Through the Lens of the Japanese Wartime Empire
Diana S. Kim

A full series listing is available at: www.cambridge.org/ESEA

For EU product safety concerns, contact us at Calle de José Abascal, 56–1°,
28003 Madrid, Spain or eugpsr@cambridge.org.

www.ingramcontent.com/pod-product-compliance
Lightning Source LLC
LaVergne TN
LVHW020352260326
834688LV00045B/1672